TRUFFLES AND OTHER CHOCOLATE CONFECTIONS

PAMELLA ASQUITH

Truffles

AND OTHER CHOCOLATE CONFECTIONS

HOLT, RINEHART AND WINSTON ··· NEW YORK

*I wish to thank the following people for their inspiration
and support: Cathy Wolfheim, Joyce Cole, Michael
Starkman, Robert Levering, Cynthia Lang, Jane Currant,
Jennifer Josephy, Robert Churchill Munson,
Marty Westerman, and all my students.*

*Library of Congress Cataloging in Publication Data
Asquith, Pamella Z.
Truffles and other chocolate confections.
Includes index.
1. Candy. 2. Cookery (Chocolate) I. Title.
TX791.A78 1984 641.8'53 83-18650
ISBN 0-03-063356-7*

First Edition

*Design by Amy Hill
Illustrations by Laura Hartman
Printed in the United States of America
1 3 5 7 9 10 8 6 4 2*

ISBN 0-03-063356-7

CONTENTS

INTRODUCTION

nly a few years ago, chocolate truffles were unknown in this country and homemade chocolate candy was largely confined to fudge. Old-fashioned fudge certainly has a place in the pantheon of chocolate confections, but anyone who has tasted Swiss, Belgian, or, more recently, American-made truffles will attest to their preeminence among chocolate creations. For sheer intensity and depth of flavor, richness, and smoothness, nothing can compare to these divine morsels. Named after the rare European fungus (*Tuber melanosporum*), the imported chocolate truffle resembles its namesake in costliness, unassuming appearance, and snob appeal. But, *homemade* chocolate truffles need not be wildly expensive or only occasional treats.

With this book, you will be able to create confections that are every bit as good as, if not better than, the finest imported products at a fraction of the cost. And while the process is somewhat exacting, the end product is well worth your efforts. Once you master the basic principles, you will find candy making surprisingly simple. You may even find yourself devising your own variations on these recipes to impress and delight your family and friends.

Also provided are recipes for other chocolate delights to round out your candy-making repertoire, including classics such as chocolate-covered caramels, toffee, and fondant, and more fanciful concoctions such as Brownie Truffles, Some-More Truffles, and an audacious and spectacular mountain made of chocolate dipped strawberries. The addition of some of these confections provides variety of color, shape, and texture to candy sampler boxes, which you probably will want to make for holiday and other gifts.

I will never forget the sensation I had biting into a truffle for the first time: the explosion of flavor, the velvety smooth texture, and deep, intense aroma! I had always been fond of chocolate (see the over one hundred chocolate cakes in my *Ultimate Chocolate Cake Book*), but suddenly I was confronted with the quintessential chocolate experience. As always when I discover something wonderful to eat, I was determined to re-create it myself and try to make it even better. Soon my friends were clamoring for more, more, more, and when I sent some truffles as a gift to my editor, Jennifer Josephy, she suggested they deserved a book all their own. Word travels fast around Berkeley, California, where I live, and friends and perfect strangers started asking me to teach classes in truffle making. Repeatedly my students, after only one class, would exclaim how simple truffles were to make. The only difficult thing about it, they said, was finding the best chocolate to use and restraining themselves from immediately eating their entire production. My students also taught me a thing or two. For instance, I learned that people with large hands find it easier to use a fork for dipping rather than their fingers. One of my students, an engineer, improvised an ingenious implement from a common meat fork found in supermarkets everywhere.

I hope by now you are eager to begin your first batch of truffles. Just a few reminders before you start—confectionery does require great attention to detail. Although simple, the art of the confectioner is not an intuitive process. For instance, the longer meat cooks, the more tender it becomes. Not so with sugar. The longer it cooks, the harder it becomes. Also, unlike baked goods, some confectionary should not be eaten freshly made but requires aging for the flavors to marry and the proper texture to be achieved. Plan ahead; timing is as crucial as the choice of fine ingredients. Precision in measuring both recipe quantities and temperature is also crucial. If you keep in mind the truffle's finicky nature, you can have great fun fabricating these little bits of heaven to present as gifts or to keep for your own indulgence and delight.

ALL ABOUT CHOCOLATE

he chocolate plant, *Theobroma cacao*, originally grew in southern Mexico and Central America. The botanical name of the plant is Latin for "food of the gods." Indeed, the Aztec Indians of Mexico considered the tree of divine origin and Quetzalcoatl, the Aztec Moon God and Gardener of Paradise, was believed to have brought the seeds earthward. Dwellers in paradise spent eternity sipping a chocolate drink under a cacao tree.

There are two main varieties of cacao tree, each producing a distinctive fruit—the criollo and the forastero. The criollo is cultivated mainly in South America. The tree is smaller, it yields a smaller crop, and its fruit ripens later than the forastero. As the criollo fruit is more delicate tasting and aromatic than the forastero, it is used only for the finest-quality chocolate and for blending. It accounts for only 10 percent of the world's production. The forastero, a hybrid grown mainly in Africa, produces a larger crop but is harsher in flavor.

Christopher Columbus was the first European to encounter cacao, in 1502 on his fourth voyage. Columbus presented Queen Isabella with some cacao beans as part of a curio collection from the New World, but she ignored them in favor of less edible booty.

In 1519 Hernando Cortez, visiting the royal court of Montezuma in Veracruz, Mexico, found that cacao was a royal beverage imbibed from golden goblets and that the beans themselves were used as money. Although he was not impressed by the taste of "chocolatl," Cortez immediately founded cacao plantations on Trinidad, Haiti, and on an island off Africa to grow this money on trees. In 1528 Cortez took his bounty back to Spain and a chocolate beverage became popular among the wealthy. The Spanish kept the methods of chocolate preparation secret and were so successful that when Dutch and English pirates captured ships laden with cacao, they hurled it overboard deriding it as "sheep's dung." The Spanish monopoly of the foodstuff lasted only until 1606 when a certain Antonio Carletti managed to introduce it into Italy. A few years later, in 1615, chocolate reached France via the royal marriage of Louis XIII and the Spanish princess Anne of Austria. Ironically, the dissemination of chocolate throughout Europe was helped along in 1569 by a papal decree of Pius V, who found the drink so disgusting that he declared, "This drink does not break the fast." Chocolate returned in a new guise to the New World in 1765 when John Hannon, an Irishman, founded a factory in New England that later became "Baker's Chocolate" and is still in operation today.

In the nineteenth century three technological advances changed chocolate from a gritty substance always served as a beverage to the smooth candy we enjoy today. In 1828 Coenraad J. van Houten, a Dutch chemist, invented the cocoa press to extract the oils or cocoa butter from the beans and developed the alkalizing process whereby cocoa is made more soluble in water. In 1875 the Swiss Henri Nestlé invented condensed milk and with Daniel Peter developed milk chocolate. In 1880 another Swiss, Rodolphe Lindt, discovered that "conching" or kneading chocolate paste and adding more cocoa butter made a smoother and tastier product. As the constant motion of the ocean waves transforms rough-edged rocks into smooth pebbles, the gritty chocolate particles are transformed by conching, so-called because Lindt's vessel for the operation was shaped like a conch shell. Today, the finest chocolate is conched as long as seventy-two hours, during which time air is also incorporated into the mixture. This air mellows and ages the chocolate, imparting the unique developed taste.

As with all other industries, chocolate has undergone major changes in the twentieth century. The day of the small family-owned company is past. Chocolate has become big business. Smaller companies have been bought up by monopolies, but even today the production of chocolate is not vertically integrated, i.e., the manufacturers do not also own the plantations. In fact most of the growers in Ghana, the region supplying the greatest proportion of raw cacao, are small farmers.

Production and consumption of chocolate have dramatically increased during this century. In 1900 production was 100,000 tons. Today the estimated production is 1,448,000 tons, about a fifteenfold increase, and chocolate seems to be increasingly popular. Chocolate-lovers congregate at chocolate festivals, every season new cookbooks are devoted exclusively to chocolate, and recently at the University of California–Berkeley, 750 students enrolled in an undergraduate course, Botany 3: Chocolate (the university expected 30). Also recently, a magic substance in chocolate has been chemically isolated and studied. Phenylethylamine, "the love drug," is the substance present in the brain when love strikes or chocolate is consumed. The chemical triggers the giddiness we associate with falling in love. Although we can now explain part of the chocolate mystique as simply a matter of chemistry, chocolate's popularity has continued to grow and the "food of the gods" will be with us, no doubt, as long as love itself.

INGREDIENTS

CHOCOLATE

O f course the most important ingredient in truffle making is chocolate. It is also the most temperamental and difficult to use. Chocolate for dipping is a highly refined and specialized product. It has a higher cocoa butter content than other eating or baking chocolate, is conched longer, and must be tempered before use (explained in full on pages 31–32). There is potential for confusion in chocolate nomenclature. Chocolate suitable for dipping may be called "dark," "bittersweet," "coating," or "dipping" chocolate. In Europe, chocolate for dipping is generally called "couverture" but in the United States there is no standard. Any chocolate that has at least 45 percent cocoa butter is suitable for dipping.

Fortunately for us in the United States, most imported chocolate is of high quality; foreign companies don't bother to export their mediocre stuff because we have plenty of that here already. A foreign label doesn't guarantee quality, but it is a good bet. The Swiss brands Lindt and Tobler, widely available at specialty stores in this country, are excellent chocolates for truffle making. The Belgian Callebaut, also available at specialty stores and by mail order, is also excellent. Peter's Dark Chocolate, made in the United States by the Nestlé Company, Krön Baking Chocolate, and Godiva Chocolate for the Kitchen are widely available and excellent. In the San Francisco Bay area where I live, Ghirardelli and Guittard chocolates are available and are very good. Bakeries and candy stores often sell chocolate in ten-pound blocks, which may be suitable for dipping. There is usually a discount when you buy in such quantity but ten pounds doesn't go very far for a serious truffler and is used up a lot more quickly than you might imagine.

Chocolate chips sold in supermarkets may produce satisfactory if not excellent results if the product is "real" chocolate and if some cocoa butter (available at pharmacies) or vegetable oil (a bland oil such as almond or safflower, 1 tablespoon to ½ pound chocolate) is added. Some chocolate chips are treated with stabilizers and will not melt; these are obviously not suitable for dipping. If you are unsure if a particular brand of chocolate is suitable for dipping, try to determine the cocoa butter content; if it is at least 45 percent, it should be fine.

SUMMER SUBSTITUTE
FOR DIPPING CHOCOLATE

As dipping chocolate begins to melt at 80°F., truffles made with it cannot be taken on a picnic or enjoyed unrefrigerated in hot weather. So-called chocolate summer coatings, in which the cocoa butter has been replaced by fats with higher melting points, such as coconut oil, are available, but in my experience they taste consistently revolting. Homemade summer coating isn't as bad, but don't expect it to taste like anything but an acceptable substitute. To make your own summer coating, buy white or vanilla summer coating and mix it with unsweetened chocolate in the proportion of one to one by weight. This summer coating need not be tempered; simply melt and it is ready for use.

MILK CHOCOLATE

Milk chocolate is manufactured in the same manner as bittersweet chocolate except that dry milk powder is added along with additional sugar. Milk chocolate made in the United States has a cheesy taste and a chewy, somewhat rubbery texture. Most mature palates prefer bittersweet chocolate, but don't turn up your nose at milk chocolate until you have had the finest Swiss variety; it is not only excellent but provides a delightful contrast to assortments of chocolate confections.

WHITE CHOCOLATE

As explained in the chapter on Ingredients, one method of processing the cacao bean is to press the solids from the fats. The solids are brown and are called cocoa powder and the fats are white (actually a beautiful pale yellow similar to freshly made butter) and are called cocoa butter. White chocolate is made from the whitish cocoa butter, sugar, dried milk, an emulsifier, and sometimes vanilla. Real white chocolate, made with pure cocoa butter, is expensive, as cocoa butter is in great demand by the cosmetic industry for its famous skin-softening properties. White chocolate is always sweeter than dark chocolate, the cocoa solids being the bitter part of the bean.

White chocolate cannot be directly substituted for dark chocolate because of the differing proportions of sugar and fat, but it can be used in any recipe for the outside coating instead of dark chocolate, and must be tempered in the same way as dark chocolate. I have specified white chocolate in those recipes where it makes for a contrast in flavor and color, such as the Mint Truffles (page 52) or when dark chocolate would overpower a subtle flavor such as rose water or orange flower water. Blanc de Blanc de Blanc Truffles (page 57) are made with white chocolate, white rum, and white raisins, and are perhaps the ultimate in a white-chocolate-lover's dream. If you are particularly fond of white chocolate, follow the formula on page 51 to invent new combinations.

As with dark chocolate, imported white chocolate is usually of high quality. Swiss Lindt and Tobler and Belgian Callebaut are excellent but there are good domestic brands as well: *Read the label carefully*. If a particular brand contains only cocoa butter, it should work well for truffles.

STORAGE OF CHOCOLATE

Chocolate is a very stable product and has excellent keeping properties under the proper conditions. The ideal storage place is characterized by an absence of certain factors: light, moisture, heat, and humidity. As explained below, chocolate is one of the most, if not *the* most, temperature-sensitive foodstuffs. Cocoa butter starts to melt at 80°F., which ruins the delicate temper the manufacturers went to so much trouble to achieve. Store chocolate in a cool, dry place, about 50°F. A wine cellar is a good place if it is not too damp. If chocolate, like wine, is subjected to temperature variations while in storage it will suffer. Chocolate will "bloom," that is, some of the cocoa butter will come to the surface in gray streaks. This is not an insurmountable problem since chocolate must always be retempered before dipping, but eventually chocolate will lose its delicate taste and texture if improperly stored.

COCOA

As explained above, cocoa is the solid part of the cocoa bean. It is sold both sweetened (sometimes called Espresso Chocolate or powdered chocolate) and unsweetened. Cocoa powder is mainly used in recipes herein as a garnish for finished truffles for an earthy look. Both sweetened and unsweetened cocoa can be used, the degree of sweetness being a personal preference. Store cocoa in a cool, dry place, well sealed. Most brands of cocoa are of excellent quality, cocoa being much easier to produce than chocolate. The European brands usually win out in terms of subtlety of taste, but all brands of cocoa I have tried are good.

BUTTER

Butter is often used in the ganache mixture to stabilize the other fats and help the truffles keep their shape. All the recipes in this book specify unsalted butter, also sometimes called sweet butter. Salted butter contains moisture absorbed by the salt, which can alter the fat–liquid ratio in the recipes, and the salty taste can overpower the delicate flavors. The best unsalted butter is made from raw milk and is available at health food stores, although it is relatively expensive. Store unsalted butter in the freezer.

CREAM AND MILK

Cream makes the ganache mixture softer and creamier—more sensual to the bite. For cooked sugar confections such as caramel, look for cream and milk with no stabilizers or homogenizing agents. When subjected to heat these foreign substances most likely will coagulate the milk or cream solids and cause them to sink to the bottom of the pan and burn. Health food stores usually carry unhomogenized milk. For making a ganache, regular ultra-pasteurized cream available at supermarkets will work, but of course the better the quality of the cream, the better the candy.

SUGAR

The sugar specified in the recipes in this book is common white granulated sugar. Powdered or confectioners' sugar usually has 3 percent cornstarch added to prevent caking and should not be used for the cooked sugar recipes. I always keep a vanilla bean in sugar so I never have to use vanilla extract. My sugar is always pleasantly aromatic. Store sugar well sealed from moisture.

CORN SYRUP AND HONEY

Corn syrup and honey are used in recipes for cooked sugar because they help prevent a recrystallization of the sugar molecule. Use light corn syrup and a mildly flavored honey like clover so as not to interfere with the other flavors in the recipe. Store corn syrup and honey well sealed. If honey has crystallized in storage, simply heat it until it is liquid.

NUTS

Nuts and chocolate are a favorite combination with almost everyone. They offer a satisfying contrast of texture and flavor. Some recipes call for very finely ground nuts, like the Chocolate-covered Marzipan (page 106) or the Hazelnut Cream Truffles (page 72), and some call for chopped nuts, like the Roasted Almond Balls (page 69). Health food stores carry high quality nuts in bulk. Buy unfumigated nuts if possible; the poison is sometimes absorbed by the fats in the nuts and tastes and smells revolting, and, of course, any poison used to kill mold is unfit for human consumption. Cashews are often treated in this manner. Smell nuts before you buy them. If they smell like insecticide or an old sock go to another store. Be especially wary when buying nuts during the summer months. Nuts are harvested in the fall and if improperly stored by wholesalers may be rancid by summer. Store nuts at a cool room temperature away from humidity. Nuts that have absorbed moisture will be soggy and turn to an unpalatable mush when ground. Nuts need not be frozen, and indeed the fats undergo chemical changes when frozen, which can make them react in unpredictable ways in recipes.

LIQUEURS AND LIQUORS

In every state except Kentucky, Tennessee, and Nevada it is illegal to sell candy with more than 1½ percent alcohol. But happily it is not illegal to make such candies for private consumption, because they are delicious indeed. Liqueurs and liquors do represent a sizable investment, but if you compare the price ounce for ounce to flavor extracts, you will find the difference negligible and you can use them for other purposes as well. Almost any liqueur or liquor marries well with chocolate, but sometimes an aging of a day or so is necessary for the flavor to develop. Also, by the same token, if you taste a ganache immediately after adding a liqueur the flavor may not seem strong enough; don't add more, the flavor will come out as the ganache cools. Store liqueurs in a cool place away from light.

FLAVORING SYRUPS

Syrups such as framboise (raspberry) or grenadine (pomegranate) are delicious in a ganache. They are so heavy, though, that they can settle and separate out of the ganache. This can be overcome by scalding the syrup along with the cream before adding the chocolate. Syrups and liqueurs go well together, the liqueurs cutting the sweetness a bit and enhancing the fruity flavors.

FLAVOR EXTRACTS AND OILS

Unfortunately the flavor of most extracts is disappointing, tasting more of the alcohol in which the flavor is dissolved than the original flavor. Flavoring oils tend to be better, but they are difficult to come by except through mail order. Be cautious using extracts and let your nose be your guide. If the extract doesn't smell good, it probably won't taste good either.

FOOD COLORING

For fondant and Royal Icing garnishes, variety of color is sometimes called for. Either the liquid food coloring available in supermarkets or the paste colors available at specialty stores can be used. To color white chocolate, it is better to use the paste colors because the liquid colors can cause the chocolate to become rubbery.

Purists can make their own food coloring with vegetables and spices, beets for red, spinach for green, and turmeric for yellow.

Cover finely chopped beets or spinach with water, bring to a boil, and then simmer until almost all the liquid has evaporated.

Squeeze the remaining liquid through a double layer of cheese-cloth and store in the refrigerator well sealed.

To make yellow coloring, first make a strong tea with turmeric, 2 tablespoons to 1 cup water, then reduce it to ¼ cup before straining through a double layer of cheesecloth. Store in the refrigerator well sealed.

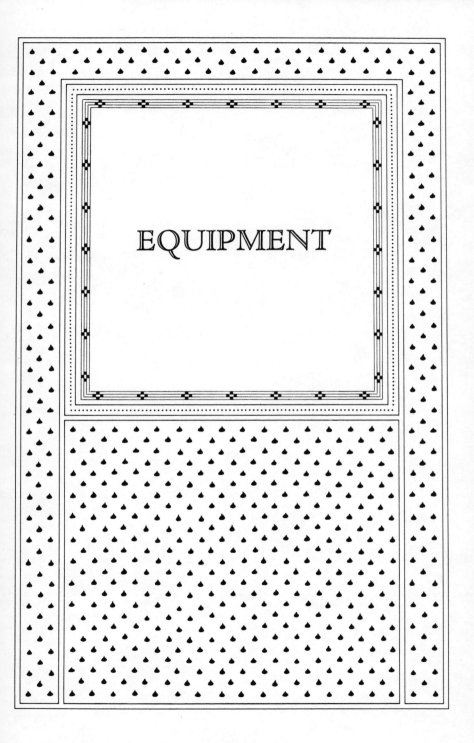

EQUIPMENT

aking truffles at home requires few pieces of equipment other than what you probably already have in your kitchen. The exceptions are a chocolate thermometer, a double boiler, and, if you want to make cooked sugar confections, a candy thermometer and a marble slab with candy rails (see Mail Order Guide, page 115).

THERMOMETERS

Chocolate and sugar are two of the most temperature-sensitive, if not *the* most temperature-sensitive, foodstuffs. One degree more or less can make the difference between successful, delicious candy and runny, rubbery sludge. Because of the drastic chemical changes that take place, chocolate and candy making are not intuitive processes as are, for instance, making soups or stews. After years of practice one may be able to learn by look or feel if chocolate or sugar is at the correct temperature, but gauging temperature with a thermometer is the only infallible method. If you are making only truffles with a ganache center, a chocolate thermometer accurately measuring between 80°F. and 110°F. is the only one you will need. However, if you also want to make caramels, fondant, toffee, or brittle, you need a candy thermometer measuring between 200°F. and 300°F. Unfortunately, these tools are expensive ($10 to $15), but the cost of one or two batches of ruined candy would probably cover the cost of the thermometer.

Chocolate thermometers are made with a metal probe to insert into the melting chocolate and a dial that registers temperature. A yogurt or yeast thermometer could double as a chocolate thermometer if it registers between 80°F. and 110°F. These tools are less expensive, usually $4 to $5.

A candy thermometer is usually a glass globe with mercury (like a fever thermometer), but it is strapped to a calibrated metal shaft. Take care the glass does not slip up or down the shaft or the reading will not be accurate.

MEASURING CUPS AND SPOONS

Accurate measurement of quantities as well as temperature is essential for successful candy making. Dented cups and spoons do not measure accurately. Glass or metal tools are preferable to plastic ones, which can absorb flavors and odors.

SCALES

Measuring chocolate by weight rather than by volume is standard procedure, as that is how it is sold. There are two kinds of scales: spring and balance. Spring scales may lose accuracy with time or abuse as the metal springs become worn and relax. Occasionally place a premeasured quantity such as a pound of butter on a spring scale to make sure it is calibrated correctly. Balance scales are usually more expensive and somewhat unwieldy, but remain totally accurate.

MIXING TOOLS

When tempering chocolate, the object is to homogenize the fats but not beat any air into the chocolate, so a chopstick or wooden spoon is the best tool. Wooden tools do not absorb heat as do metal tools. For mixing chocolate into a ganache after the cream has been scalded, a wire whisk is the best tool to use because it incorporates the mixture very quickly.

KNIVES AND CUTTING BOARDS

For best results, chocolate must be very finely chopped before being melted or tempered. This is a somewhat tedious process (and one that unfortunately cannot be overcome by using a food processor, as explained below) but one that is made easier with the proper knife. Use a Chinese cleaver or a French chopping knife. A cleaver has an advantage in that you can pick up the chopped chocolate and transfer it to the double boiler directly on the blade of the knife.

Have a separate cutting board for chocolate. I usually chop chocolate on my marble slab to make sure it doesn't absorb the garlic and other flavors that are thoroughly impregnated in my wooden board. Nothing dulls a knife faster than cutting on marble, though, so this method requires extra maintenance, but I think it is worth it.

GRATERS

Chocolate can be grated as well as chopped before being tempered, but sometimes grated chocolate can pick up so much static electricity that it practically jumps all over the room. Use a box grater or a hand-cranked nut grater. Chocolate cannot be properly chopped or grated in a food processor or electric blender as the heat produced by the friction causes it to melt and then set prematurely.

SCRAPERS AND SPATULAS

Rubber and metal scrapers and spatulas in various shapes and sizes are good to have in a chocolatier's kitchen. Chocolate crumbs pressed into a cutting board, on the floor, or elsewhere, can be more easily scraped off than washed off. Scrapers can also double as fondant paddles.

PALETTE KNIVES

Palette knives have a thin and flexible blade with a rounded tip. Offset or elbow palette knives are helpful to reach into difficult places, such as dislodging the first piece of fudge in a rimmed pan.

FOOD PROCESSORS

Food processors are used to grind nuts but should not be used to grate chocolate, as mentioned above.

MANUAL NUT AND CHOCOLATE GRATERS

Old-fashioned-looking, hand-cranked nut graters are ideal for grating chocolate before tempering. The texture produced is very fine, dry, and even. Thoroughly dry the grating drum after washing because it can rust very quickly.

Small hand-held graters can also grate chocolate, although only a small amount can be grated at a time.

MORTAR AND PESTLE

A mortar and pestle is used to grind spices for truffle making.

DOUBLE BOILERS

As chocolate is too delicate to be melted over direct heat, a double boiler or bain-marie is essential for truffle making. A double boiler can be improvised by placing a bowl or pan within a larger pan but the top part must fit snugly or you must make a foil collar for the bottom pan. If any steam from the bottom condenses on the melting chocolate, it may become rubbery and impossible to work with. When tempering chocolate, do not place the lid on the double boiler, as moisture can condense on it and thus contaminate the chocolate.

SAUCEPANS

Heavy saucepans are used to scald cream for making ganache and to cook sugar. Cast-iron saucepans coated with enamel are very good, as are stainless steel or plain cast iron. Remember that cream and cooking sugar boil up to six times their cold volume, so be sure to use a large enough saucepan.

A MARBLE SLAB AND CANDY RAILS

A 12-by-12-inch marble slab is good to have for cooked sugar work. Chocolate sticks to marble, so don't put unset truffles on it. A piece of formica, plastic, or a heavy baking sheet can be substituted for marble, but these materials can warp. Marble is surprisingly inexpensive, doesn't warp, and lasts forever, so it is a good investment as well as the best piece of equipment for candy making. A used building supply or architectural salvage store may have large pieces of marble at a relatively inexpensive price.

Candy rails are bars of iron or plastic used on a marble slab to regulate the thickness of cooked candy as it cools. Iron rails are very expensive and difficult to find in stores, but the plastic variety are cheap and available by mail order (see page 115). An advantage of using rails is that once the candy is set and the rails are removed, the shape of the pieces is not deformed by prying them out of a rimmed pan.

DIPPING FORKS

When my students ask me what my favorite dipping fork is, I hold up my index and middle fingers in Winston Churchill's "victory" sign. A dipping fork is not an essential piece of equipment in a chocolatier's *batterie de cuisine*, since finger-dipping can be very fast and clean after a little practice. However, if your hands are very large, a fork may make dipping easier for you. Professional

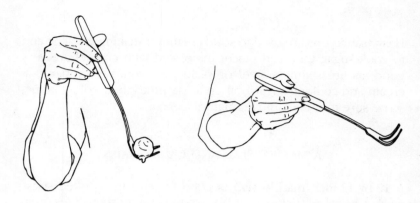

dipping forks are available by mail order (page 115) or you can use a two-pronged meat fork. Dipping forks are easy to make by bending the tines of an inexpensive lightweight aluminum meat fork available at supermarkets, or you can fashion one from an unpainted coat hanger.

PEELER

A vegetable peeler is used to make shaved chocolate as a garnish for truffles.

MELON BALLER

A melon baller can be used to form ganache into balls for dipping, but a regular teaspoon is also fine for the job.

MOLDS AND SQUEEZE BOTTLES

Chocolate molds of clear plastic are widely available in myriad sizes and shapes. There are two kinds of molds: flat-backed and two-piece (used to create a free-standing object such as a rabbit or Santa Claus). If I have any leftover dipping chocolate, I usually pour it directly into a mold, so I always have lots of shapes available to fill an odd corner in a candy box, to garnish a cake, or just for fun. Molds need no special care, just a little washing, but not in a dishwasher, which can melt them. Store molds in such a way that they do not get dented or bent out of shape.

Squeeze bottles (like those used in restaurants for catsup and mustard) make chocolate molding easy and nonmessy. Extra chocolate can be stored and actually retempered in the bottles (set the bottle in a pan of hot water) whenever needed.

ELECTRIC FRYING PAN

An electric frying pan filled with water and turned on LOW may be ideal for melting chocolate. Put the chocolate in a bowl and make a foil collar between the bowl and the side of the frying pan to cover the water so none of it condenses on the chocolate. Junk stores always seem to have lots of used electric frying pans for a few dollars.

PASTRY BAGS AND TIPS

Pastry bags are used to make garnishes for truffles. Truffles can be threaded using a pastry bag and a plain round writing tip (page 41). Icing flowerets or leaves can be made by using flower and leaf tips. Pastry bags come in several materials: canvas, rubber-coated canvas, plastic, nylon, and paper. I prefer the most light-weight and flexible bags in nylon and disposable plastic (available by mail order, page 115).

STORAGE CONTAINERS

Tin boxes in which imported butter cookies and fruitcakes are packed make excellent storage containers for truffles, because they are completely air- and watertight. Otherwise, place truffles in plastic containers with snap-on lids or wrap in plastic bags. Ziplock bags are especially secure. When completely set, truffles can be stacked one on top of another without being crushed, so it isn't necessary to have a storage container with layers.

CONFECTIONERS' FOIL

Special lightweight foil, usually found in gold, red, blue, and green, is available for wrapping candy. It is not necessary to wrap each truffle individually in foil, but it can provide color variation in a candy box. Chocolate-covered Cherries (page 96) should be wrapped in foil to keep the cherry liquor from seeping out.

WAX OR PARCHMENT PAPER

Regular wax or special siliconized parchment paper is essential for truffle making. Unset truffles are placed on this paper because chocolate does not stick to it, as it does to marble or ceramic plates. Parchment is available at specialty cookware stores or by mail order (page 115).

CASEMENT OR CANDY CUPS

Fluted paper casement or candy cups beautifully set off truffles in a candy box or on a platter. They are available in a variety of colors: brown, red, white, pastels, and flowered prints. Personally I think that red cups make for the most dramatic and beautiful contrast to dark chocolate. Variety stores or dime stores sometimes carry candy cups, or perhaps your local candy store will sell some. They are also available by mail order (page 115).

CANDY BOXES

Any shallow box can be used as a candy box. Special candy boxes are sold in variety stores or by mail order. For a special touch, you can even have candy boxes imprinted with your name.

TECHNIQUES

MAKING GANACHE

T he truffle center mixture is called ganache and is easy to make. It is made of chocolate with some added fat, such as butter and/or cream for smoothness, and flavorings, such as liqueurs.

For a cream-based ganache, you don't even need a double boiler; the cream is scalded in a saucepan, then removed from the heat, and the chocolate and other ingredients are added. When scalding the cream, watch closely; the cream boils up very quickly and will make a formidable mess on your stove top if it is not removed from the heat in time. Stir the chocolate in quickly and vigorously until completely melted. A wire whisk is a good tool to use for this task. Allow the ganache to cool to 110°F. before adding any alcohol-based flavors; alcohol is volatile above 110°F. Any heavy syrup such as framboise should be scalded with the cream or it will separate and sink to the bottom of the ganache as it cools.

If you taste a warm ganache, it may not seem strongly flavored enough, but the flavors will develop and intensify as it cools.

The ganache should be poured into another container to set, because sometimes unmelted chocolate can sink to the bottom and lodge in the corners of a saucepan. Most ganaches will set in 4 hours in the refrigerator. The shallower the container into which it is poured, the faster it will set. Ganache can be made a day or even a week ahead of time. Indeed, the flavors will mellow and ripen with age, so it is best to plan ahead.

FORMING BALLS

When the ganache has set, the next step is to form the balls or centers for dipping. Have a platter or baking sheet lined with wax

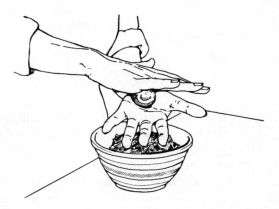

or parchment paper ready to receive the formed balls. Spoon out the ganache. Approximately one tablespoonful will form a ¾-inch-diameter ball. Roll it between your palms until it is round. If it is too soft, return the ganache to the refrigerator, or spoon out the balls, but don't form them; refrigerate and then form.

Before being dipped, the balls should be placed in the freezer. The objective here is not actually to freeze the balls but to form a slight skin or crust that makes the dipping easier. The balls should be no colder than 55°F. when dipped or the chocolate coating will crack, or an unsightly little geyser of the ganache will break through the coating. About 10 minutes in the freezer should be sufficient to form the skin but not make the balls too cold for dipping. They needn't be wrapped for this brief freezing period.

If you don't have time to dip the balls right away, wrap them in plastic and store them in the freezer, but remember to let them come to 55°F. before dipping. To save on cleanup time, make several flavors of ganache, form into balls, freeze them for storage, and then dip them all at once.

WHY CHOCOLATE MUST BE TEMPERED

Tempering is the process whereby all the fats in chocolate are melted and stabilized before the chocolate cools and sets.

Cocoa butter is a complex molecule made from many lipid (fat) compounds, each of which melts and sets at a different temperature. Chocolate may seem like the devil incarnate until you know how to temper it properly, and poor tempering is the downfall of many an otherwise careful chocolatier. Poorly tempered chocolate can "bloom," that is, the cocoa butter separates, causing gray streaks through the chocolate. Poorly tempered chocolate will not have a beautiful patina and crisp snap when bitten into.

Some of the fats in chocolate start to melt at 80°F., but all of them aren't melted until it reaches 104°F. The fact that chocolate is fairly liquid by 96°F. is deceptive, because if the chocolate is not brought to 104°F. these higher melting fats cannot be properly reincorporated with the lower melting fats as the chocolate sets, causing "bloom." But, if the chocolate is heated to higher than 110°F., the fats go into what is called the "beta-crystal stage" and the chocolate is ruined for all delicate work like dipping. To further complicate matters, the chocolate must be cooled to 80°F. and then reheated for dipping. Some chocolatiers dogmatically insist that 89°F. is the only proper temperature for dipping. I have found that there is usually a range of temperatures from 85° to 92°F. at which most chocolate will be best for dipping, and the exact temperature can vary from chocolate to chocolate. All chocolates I have worked with do respond well to 89°F., so if you are the kind of person most comfortable with an absolute number, 89°F. is it. This narrow range of temperatures between success and utter (not partial) failure makes a good thermometer a chocolatier's best friend.

HOW TO TEMPER CHOCOLATE

Large industrial chocolate tempering machines exist for commercial candy makers. Perhaps someday soon, because of the great public interest in chocolate, a small home version will be available, but in the meantime, we must be content with the old-fashioned hard way.

Start by chopping the chocolate very finely. Throughout the

tempering process be careful that no moisture gets into or condenses on the chocolate or it will become rubbery and difficult if not impossible to work with. As you chop the chocolate, don't grip the knife so tightly that your hands sweat, as even this minuscule amount of moisture can ruin chocolate.

Place the chopped chocolate in the top of an absolutely dry double boiler over hot, but not even simmering, water. A good rule is to never let the water get above 130°F. Stir the chocolate as it melts. A chopstick is my favorite tool for this task.

Heat the chocolate to 104°F. Remove the top from the bottom of the double boiler. Cover the bottom of the double boiler so steam escaping from it does not have a chance to condense on the chocolate. Cool the chocolate to 80°F. (stirring occasionally). Return the top of the double boiler with the chocolate to the bottom and bring the chocolate back up to 89°F. (stirring occasionally). This process may take 10 to 15 minutes.

WHAT TO DO IF DIPPING CHOCOLATE TURNS RUBBERY

As I've probably mentioned ten times by now, moisture is the culprit responsible for this phenomenon. Either steam from the bottom of the double boiler condensed on the chocolate, there was too much humidity in the air, or your hands were clammy. Different chocolates respond to different "doctors." First, try a little cocoa butter (available at pharmacies), unsalted butter, or a bland vegetable oil such as almond or safflower (1 tablespoon to ½ pound chocolate). If this doesn't work, ironically, adding a teaspoon *more* water may. Not all kinds of chocolate respond to the water "doctor," so try it only as a last resort.

WHAT TO DO IF DIPPING CHOCOLATE TURNS GRITTY

At temperatures over 110°F., chocolate goes from the "alpha-crystal stage" to the "beta-crystal stage." In other words, you blew it! Burned it actually, and there is nothing you can do to return it

PROBLEMS AND CAUSES OF UNSUCCESSFUL DIPPED CHOCOLATES

CAUSE	Gray streaks, "bloom" (separation of cocoa butter)	Tiny white spots	Cloudiness	Graininess	Brittleness	Foot*	Rubbery dipping chocolate	After setting, chocolate coating cracks	Geysers of ganache burst through coating
Water condensing on or otherwise contaminating dipping chocolate							X		
Excess humidity in room while dipping or in storage		X	X				X		
Chocolate not stirred enough while tempering or while dipping	X								
Beta-crystal stage; chocolate heated higher than 110°F. while tempering		X		X	X				
Chocolate not heated high enough while tempering	X								
Excess chocolate not allowed to drip off before placing truffles on the paper to set						X			
Temperature too high while dipping						X			
Temperature too low while dipping	X					X			
Temperature variation too extreme while in storage	X								
Room too hot; chocolate set too slowly	X		X						
Room too cool; chocolate set too quickly			X						
Center too cold for dipping								X	X

*Garden sluglike aberration

to the alpha stage. You can, however, make a ganache with up to half the recipe amount of betaized chocolate (5 ounces in a recipe calling for 10 ounces of chocolate), so you needn't throw it out, just don't try to use it for dipping.

ABOUT DIPPING

Ideally, dipping should be done in a cool room, 60° to 65°F., with low humidity. In warmer months, work at night or in the early morning. Before dipping, it is a good idea to line your entire work area with wax or parchment paper. Nothing is messier than chocolate, and you will be thankful at cleanup time to simply crumple up the soiled paper and dispose of it. Remember to stir the chocolate occasionally as you are dipping to equalize the temperature. Speed is important when dipping because if the center becomes too warm, it will be too soft to dip. Practice dipping walnut halves or Brazil nuts to acquire rhythm and speed. Dipping goes faster than you might think. It should take no more than 10 seconds to dip a center after a little practice; that's a rate of 30 in 5 minutes. Tempering the chocolate and cleaning up take much longer than the actual dipping.

Most recipes in this book specify 1 to 1¼ pounds of chocolate to dip 35 centers. Not all the chocolate is used, but you must melt at least 1 to 1¼ pounds in order to cover the centers easily. Scrape any excess, probably 3 to 4 ounces, onto wax or parchment paper to harden or make molds of it. I always mold my leftover dipping chocolate; and I can remelt the chocolate if necessary. Have a flat platter or baking sheet lined with wax or parchment paper ready to receive the dipped truffles.

ABOUT HAND-DIPPING

If you tend toward clammy hands, use a dipping fork (remember chocolate and moisture don't mix). Also, people with very large hands may find it easier to use a dipping fork than their fingers.

There are two methods of hand-dipping: the centers can be dipped directly into the chocolate in the double boiler, or the chocolate can be poured onto a marble slab a bit at a time and the centers rolled in it. The advantage of the first method is that there is one less piece of equipment to clean, but with the second method it is easier to keep the chocolate tempered because the constant agitation equalizes the temperature.

DOUBLE BOILER METHOD OF HAND-DIPPING

1. Drop the center into the chocolate. Using only two fingers—the index and middle—pull the chocolate up to cover the center and quickly lift it up between your two fingers in a scooping motion. This procedure should take no more than 2 seconds.

2. Tap the excess chocolate off the truffle and your fingers; otherwise your truffle will have a "foot" and look like a garden slug.

3. Invert the dipped truffle onto the wax or parchment paper. As it slips off your fingers, as a final gesture, make a swirl with the last stringy bit of chocolate.

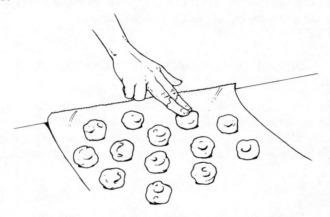

4. Allow the dipped truffles to set up or harden without touching them. In a 60° to 65°F. low humidity room they will partially set in 3 minutes, but don't touch them for at least 15 minutes; if you do, your fingerprints will blemish them. If the truffles do not seem set after 10 minutes, the room is either too hot or too humid. Put them into the refrigerator uncovered. Chocolate has a nicer patina if allowed to cool at room temperature, so don't refrigerate the truffles unless you must.

Refer to page 33 for problems and causes of unsuccessful dipped chocolates.

MARBLE SLAB METHOD OF HAND-DIPPING

1. Pour about ½ cup of the tempered chocolate onto the slab. Work it back and forth with your index, middle, and ring fingers

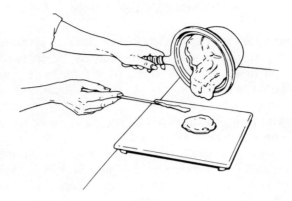

as you would palette paint or plaster. Drop the center into the puddle of chocolate and pull chocolate around and over it. Quickly lift it up between your index and middle fingers in a scooping motion. Pour more chocolate onto the marble after dipping 4 to 5 centers, or as need be. Constantly palette the chocolate as you're dipping to equalize the temperature.

Steps 2, 3, and 4 are the same as for the Double Boiler Method.

DIPPING FORK METHOD

Have a depth of at least 1½ inches of chocolate in the double boiler.

1. Balance the center on the edge of the fork. Submerge it in the chocolate and then lift it out.

2. Tap the fork against the side of the double boiler to remove the excess chocolate and prevent the garden slug foot.

3. Invert the dipped chocolate onto the wax or parchment paper and as it slips off the fork, make a swirl with one tine as decoration.

Follow Step 4 as in the Double Boiler Hand-dipping Method.

COOKING SUGAR

To expand your repertory of chocolate confections from simple ganache-based truffles to enrobed caramels, toffee, fondant, and brittles, you first must understand what happens to sugar as it cooks. The basis of all these confections is sugar and sugar is a crystal. The crystals of granulated sugar are large and unevenly shaped. When sugar is dissolved in water and cooked, the crystalline structure changes. As it cools, several new structures are possible. It can recrystallize into exceedingly small and evenly shaped crystals (as in fudge or fondant), very large and evenly shaped crystals (as in rock candy), or recrystallization can be completely prevented (as in caramel). This range of chemical changes makes sugar a unique and fascinating foodstuff to work with, but one with which you must be as precise and rigorous as a scientist. Some people are not temperamentally suited to be confectioners, finding such fastidious attention to detail irritating. The rules of confectionery are, like the rules of mathematics, immutable. If a recipe specifies that sugar be cooked to 238°F., it means 238° exactly, not 236° or 241°. By the same token, the measurement of the quantities must be exact. The words "almost" and "about" are not part of a confectioner's vocabulary. Humidity is also a factor greatly affecting candy making, but unfortunately one that cannot be controlled. On rainy or humid days it may not be possible to make candy successfully.

The following is a chart of the different forms sugar takes after reaching certain temperatures.

FORM	TEMPERATURE F.	COLD WATER TEST
Fudge or Fondant	236° to 238°	Soft ball
Caramel	246° to 250°	Firm ball
Torrone	250° to 252°	Hard ball
Toffee	290° to 300°	Soft crack
Brittle	300°	Hard crack

The cold water test is used by some experienced confectioners and is based on what sugar does when dropped into cold water at a certain temperature. I do not recommend this method for beginners because your own judgment of what constitutes a soft vs. firm vs. hard ball may not be what a confectioner means by soft, firm, or hard, and also by the time you have completed the test, the sugar may have cooked more and risen a degree or two in temperature. The initial cost of a candy thermometer will probably be less than a few batches of ruined candy and prevents the frustration of not knowing exactly what went wrong.

The ways in which sugar is manipulated at certain temperatures also affect the outcome of the candy. For instance, if fudge or fondant is beaten before it has cooled, it will be gritty, but if beaten at 110°F, it will be creamy and smooth. Also, if you try to take shortcuts in a recipe by not wiping away any undissolved sugar crystals, the candy will not recrystallize properly as it cools. Follow the recipe procedures exactly.

FINE POINTS OF COOKING SUGAR

1. Measure ingredients exactly.

2. Measure temperatures exactly.

3. Follow procedures outlined exactly.

4. When reading the thermometer, your eye should be at the same level as the mercury in the tube.

5. Do not boil water or make stock while you are making candy.

6. If your tap water is extremely alkaline, use distilled water.

7. Make sure your saucepan is at least 6 times larger than the volume of the sugar syrup; it will "boil up."

8. If you live more than 1,000 feet above sea level, subtract 1 degree for every thousand feet in calculating sugar temperatures.

9. On a humid or rainy day, make soup not candy.

10. Use only the freshest milk or cream; sour milk will curdle as it cooks.

ROLLING TRUFFLES IN COCOA

Some truffles, both dipped and undipped, are rolled in cocoa as a garnish for a finished, earthy look. You may use either sweetened or unsweetened cocoa. The cocoa need not be sifted. Simply

place some (½ cup should be plenty for 40 truffles) in a bowl, drop the truffle in, and roll it around a bit until it is completely covered with cocoa. Truffles that have been frozen may have absorbed their cocoa; if so, simply reroll them before serving.

GARNISHING TRUFFLES

Truffles are attractive even without a garnish, but to differentiate among many different kinds of truffles or just for fun, there are many ways to garnish them. Suggested optional garnishes are included in many recipes, but feel free to invent your own combinations. Place a garnish on top of a truffle when the chocolate has only half set to make sure it will stick.

Easy and simple garnishes include:

The harlequin effect: after dipped truffles have set, dip half of them again in a contrasting color chocolate: white and bittersweet, bittersweet and milk, or white and milk.

Threading: after dipped truffles have set, make threadlike streaks by placing chocolate in a pastry bag fitted with a plain writing tip and moving it back and forth over the truffles. Use the same kind or a contrasting color of chocolate.

Nuts: whole blanched or unblanched almonds, half walnuts or pecans, chopped nuts sprinkled on top (½ cup for 40 truffles), or chopped nuts pressed into the entire truffle (1 cup for 40 truffles).

Chocolate coffee beans: sometimes called Mocha Beans.

Candied citrus rind: (page 112).

Coconut: sprinkled on top (½ cup for 40 truffles).

Crystallized ginger: available at gourmet stores.

Edible glitter: wonderful and zany stuff made of gum arabic and food color (available by mail order).

Chocolate sprinkles or jimmies: these usually taste of paraffin, if they have a taste at all, but it is possible to find good ones.

Candied violets or rose petals: available at gourmet stores or make your own, page 112.

Royal Icing flowerets: (page 111).

Shaved chocolate: with a vegetable peeler, make small chocolate curls by shaving off a block of chocolate.

STORING TRUFFLES

The individual recipes specify storage instructions, but generally chocolate confections should be stored in the refrigerator. Any confections that can be refrigerated can also be frozen and should be if they are to be kept more than 2 weeks. Wrap them well in plastic.

FREEZING TRUFFLES

Both dipped and undipped truffles can be successfully frozen. The temper of the dipped chocolate should not be affected, if the dipping has been properly done to begin with. Double-wrap the truffles in plastic bags very securely, pressing out all the air from the bag. It is a good idea to place the wrapped truffles in a rigid container, because they can be accidentally crushed if pushed against less malleable objects in the freezer.

Cooked sugar confections are not suitable for freezing; they lose texture and flavor. Some of the recipes in the chapter on Other Chocolate Confections, however, can be successfully frozen, as indicated.

I have frozen truffles for up to 3 months with no signs of deterioration. If you have a self-defrosting freezer that works on the principle of melting the accumulated ice daily, be vigilant; if the truffles thaw and then refreeze often, they will suffer.

MAILING TRUFFLES

Once you have mastered the art of truffle making, you will want to send them to all your friends and relatives. During the cool winter months, this is no problem. Simply pack them in such a way that they do not get knocked around in the box. It is a good idea to double-dip truffles to be mailed to make them more crush-resistant. Unfortunately, truffles should not be mailed during the warm summer months. When the temperature climbs over 80°F., chocolate begins to melt, and the beautiful temper is ruined.

EATING TRUFFLES!

Although truffles should be stored refrigerated, they should be eaten at room temperature for a full bouquet of aroma and flavor. Let them sit at room temperature at least 30 minutes before ingesting.

GANACHE-BASED DIPPED TRUFFLES

Ganache Truffles I

This formula for a medium-bodied ganache uses both cream and butter. You may add any liquid flavoring.

1 cup whipping cream
12 ounces bittersweet chocolate, very finely chopped
5 tablespoons unsalted butter, room temperature
1/4 cup liquid (coffee, liqueur, syrup)
....
1 1/4 pounds bittersweet chocolate for dipping

1. In a heavy 1½- to 2-quart saucepan, scald the cream. Remove from the heat and quickly stir in the chocolate until completely melted. (If you are using a syrup, add it to the cream before scalding.)

2. Cool 5 minutes and stir in the butter and liquid.

3. Cover and refrigerate until set, about 4 hours or overnight.

4. Form into tablespoon-sized balls and freeze for 10 minutes (see Techniques).

5. Temper the chocolate and dip each ball into it (see Techniques).

6. Store well sealed in the refrigerator or freezer.

POSSIBLE
FLAVORINGS

Brandy or cognac
Calvados
Cassis or grenadine
Drambuie, Scotch, or whiskey
Port or sherry
Madeira or sweet vermouth

Espresso
Kirschwasser or rum
1 tablespoon malt extract and 3 tablespoons coffee
Honey

Ganache Truffles II

40 ONE-INCH
DIAMETER
TRUFFLES

This formula for ganache uses only chocolate and cream. It is more light-bodied than Ganache I.

1 cup whipping cream
12 ounces bittersweet chocolate, very finely chopped
1 tablespoon liquid (coffee, liqueur, syrup)

1¼ pounds bittersweet chocolate for dipping

1. In a heavy 1½- to 2-quart saucepan, scald the cream. Remove from the heat and quickly stir in the chocolate until completely melted. (If you are using a syrup, add it to the cream before scalding.) Cool 5 minutes, then add the liquid.

2. Cover and refrigerate until set, about 4 hours or overnight.

3. Form into tablespoon-sized balls and freeze for 10 minutes (see Techniques).

4. Temper the chocolate and dip each ball into it (see Techniques).

5. Store well sealed in the refrigerator or freezer.

Ganache Truffles III

40 ONE-INCH
DIAMETER
TRUFFLES

This ganache is similar to Ganache II except it is denser and therefore somewhat easier for a beginning dipper to work with.

1 cup whipping cream
14 ounces bittersweet chocolate, very finely chopped
2 tablespoons liquid (coffee, liqueur, syrup)

1¼ pounds bittersweet chocolate for dipping

Follow the procedures for Ganache II.
These truffles are suitable for freezing.

Ganache Truffles IV

25 ONE-INCH
DIAMETER
TRUFFLES

This ganache made with sweetened condensed milk is neither cheaper nor easier than a ganache made with real cream. Its texture is similar to milk chocolate.

8 ounces bittersweet chocolate, very finely chopped
¾ cup sweetened condensed milk
1 tablespoon liquid (coffee, liqueur, syrup)

1 pound milk chocolate or bittersweet chocolate for dipping

1. In the top of a double boiler, over hot but not simmering water, melt the chocolate. Stir in the milk and liquid.

2. Cover and refrigerate until set, about 4 hours or overnight.

3. Form into tablespoon-sized balls and freeze for 10 minutes (see Techniques).

4. Temper the chocolate and dip each ball into it (see Techniques).

5. Store well sealed in the refrigerator or freezer.

Milk Chocolate Ganache Truffles

32 ONE-INCH
DIAMETER
TRUFFLES

This formula uses milk chocolate and is somewhat sweeter than those using bittersweet chocolate.

½ cup whipping cream
12 ounces milk chocolate, very finely chopped
3 tablespoons unsalted butter
1 tablespoon liquid (coffee or syrup; liqueur and
*   milk chocolate are an incongruous combination)*

1 pound milk chocolate for dipping

1. In a heavy 1½- to 2-quart saucepan, scald the cream. Remove from the heat and quickly stir in the chocolate until completely melted. Cool 5 minutes, then stir in the butter and liquid.

2. Cover and refrigerate until set, about 4 hours or overnight.

3. Form into tablespoon-sized balls and freeze for 10 minutes (see Techniques).

4. Temper the chocolate and dip each ball into it (see Techniques).

5. Store well sealed in the refrigerator or freezer.

White Chocolate Ganache

24 ONE-INCH
DIAMETER
TRUFFLES

This formula for ganache uses only cream because butter would color it. Use a colorless liquid if you want the ganache to remain white.

⅓ cup whipping cream
8 ounces white chocolate, very finely chopped
1 tablespoon liquid (clear liqueur such as
*   kirschwasser, white rum, or eau de vie)*

1 pound white or bittersweet chocolate for dipping

1. In a heavy 1½- to 2-quart saucepan, scald the cream. Remove from the heat and quickly stir in the chocolate until completely melted. Cool 5 minutes and stir in the liquid.

2. Cover and refrigerate until set, about 4 hours or overnight.

3. Form into tablespoon-sized balls and freeze for 10 minutes (see Techniques).

4. Temper the chocolate and dip each ball into it (see Techniques).

5. Store well sealed in the refrigerator or freezer.

Mint Truffles

36 ONE-INCH
DIAMETER
TRUFFLES

The ultimate in after-dinner mints.

1 cup whipping cream
12 ounces bittersweet chocolate, very finely chopped
2 tablespoons liquid (¼ teaspoon mint extract and
  kirschwasser, water, or coffee, or 1 tablespoon
  crème de menthe and 1 tablespoon kirschwasser)

1¼ pounds white chocolate for dipping

1. In a heavy 1½- to 2-quart saucepan, scald the cream. Remove from the heat and quickly stir in the chocolate until smooth, then add the liquid. Cover and refrigerate until set, about 4 hours or overnight.

2. Form into tablespoon-sized balls and freeze for 10 minutes (see Techniques).

3. Temper the chocolate and dip each ball into it (see Techniques).

4. Store well sealed in the refrigerator or freezer.

OPTIONAL
GARNISHES

Threads of bittersweet chocolate (page 41)
36 green Royal Icing leaves (page 111)
Dip half in dark chocolate for a harlequin effect (page 41)

Rum Raisin Truffles

36 ONE-INCH DIAMETER TRUFFLES

Almost any combination of liqueur and dried fruit is delicious, but especially rum and raisins.

¼ cup rum, either light or dark
¾ cup raisins
1 cup whipping cream
12 ounces bittersweet chocolate, very finely chopped
3 tablespoons unsalted butter

1¼ pounds bittersweet chocolate for dipping

1. Pour the rum over the raisins and allow them to steep at least an hour or overnight.

2. In a heavy 1½- to 2-quart saucepan, scald the cream. Remove from the heat and quickly stir in the chocolate until completely melted. Cool 5 minutes, then add the rum-soaked raisins, any unabsorbed rum, and butter.

3. Cover and refrigerate until set, about 4 hours or overnight.

4. Form into tablespoon-sized balls and freeze for 10 minutes (see Techniques).

5. Temper the chocolate and dip each ball into it (see Techniques).

6. Store well wrapped in the refrigerator or freezer.

VARIATIONS

Substitute figs and cognac, prunes and brandy, dates and kirschwasser, or apples and calvados for the rum and raisins.

OPTIONAL GARNISHES

Roll in cocoa
Threads of bittersweet chocolate (page 41)

Strawberry Truffles

36 ONE-INCH
DIAMETER
TRUFFLES

Very fruity and juicy.

1 cup whipping cream
12 ounces bittersweet chocolate, very finely chopped
*1/2 cup thick strawberry jam (strain if necessary to
    eliminate excess liquid)*
1/4 cup kirschwasser
1/4 cup unsalted butter

1 1/4 pounds bittersweet chocolate for dipping

1. In a heavy 1 1/2- to 2-quart saucepan, scald the cream. Remove from the heat and quickly stir in the chocolate until melted. Cool 5 minutes, then add the jam, kirschwasser, and butter.

2. Cover and refrigerate until set, about 4 hours or overnight.

3. Form into balls and freeze for 10 minutes (see Techniques).

4. Temper the chocolate and dip each ball into it (see Techniques).

5. Store well wrapped in the refrigerator or freezer.

VARIATIONS   Use any flavor fruit jam, strained.

OPTIONAL   Roll the dipped truffles in cocoa
GARNISHES   36 strawberry candies, sometimes called pastilles
    (available at gourmet stores)

Ambrosial Balls

40 THREE-
QUARTER-INCH
DIAMETER
TRUFFLES

These truffles feature tropical fruit, rum, and nuts and may be simply rolled in coconut or dipped in chocolate.

1 cup whipping cream
10 ounces bittersweet chocolate, very finely chopped
3 tablespoons rum
½ cup unsweetened dried coconut
½ cup macadamia nuts or almonds, roasted and chopped
¼ cup dried banana chips, chopped (optional)
¼ cup dried pineapple, chopped

1 pound bittersweet or white chocolate for dipping, or
1 cup unsweetened dried coconut

1. In a heavy 1½- to 2-quart saucepan, scald the cream. Remove from heat and quickly stir in the chocolate until smooth. Cool 5 minutes, then add the rum, coconut, nuts, and fruit. Cover and refrigerate until set, about 4 hours or overnight.

2. Form into tablespoon-sized balls.

3. For dipped truffles: Freeze for 10 minutes. Temper the chocolate and dip the balls into it (see Techniques).

4. For undipped truffles: Roll the balls in the coconut.

5. Store well sealed in the refrigerator or freezer.

OPTIONAL
GARNISH

40 one-eighth-inch squares dried pineapple

Cream Cheese Ganache Truffles

24 ONE-INCH
DIAMETER
TRUFFLES

These truffles have a slightly tart taste and a very creamy and smooth texture.

6 ounces cream cheese, room temperature
6 ounces bittersweet chocolate, very finely chopped
¼ cup honey

1 pound bittersweet chocolate for dipping

1. In the top of a double boiler over hot, but not simmering, water, melt the chocolate and honey. Fold in the softened cream cheese and stir until no lumps remain.

2. Cover and refrigerate until set, about 4 hours or overnight.

3. Form into tablespoon-sized balls and freeze for 10 minutes (see Techniques).

4. Temper the chocolate and dip each ball into it (see Techniques).

5. Store well sealed in the refrigerator or freezer.

OPTIONAL
GARNISHES

Threads of white chocolate (page 41)
Dip half in white chocolate for a harlequin effect
(page 41)

Blanc de Blanc de Blanc Truffles

27 ONE-INCH
DIAMETER
TRUFFLES

White chocolate, white raisins, and white rum are featured in these dainties.

½ cup white raisins
3 tablespoons white rum
10 ounces white chocolate, very finely chopped
⅓ cup whipping cream

1 pound white chocolate for dipping

1. Allow the raisins to steep in the rum for at least 1 hour or overnight.

2. In the top of a double boiler, over hot but not simmering water, melt the chocolate in the cream. Stir in the raisins and rum. Cover and refrigerate until set, about 4 hours or overnight.

3. Form into tablespoon-sized balls and freeze for 10 minutes (see Techniques).

4. Temper the chocolate and dip the balls into it (see Techniques).

5. Store well sealed in the refrigerator or freezer.

OPTIONAL
GARNISH

Place a white raisin on top of each truffle when the coating is almost set

Rose Water Truffles

24 ONE-INCH
DIAMETER
TRUFFLES

A taste for rose water is an acquired one. At first it may seem strange, but many people find it pleasing. It is available at Middle Eastern groceries.

8 ounces white chocolate, very finely chopped
½ cup whipping cream
½ teaspoon rose essence concentrate

1 pound white or bittersweet chocolate for dipping

1. In the top of a double boiler, over hot but not simmering water, melt the chocolate. Stir in the cream and rose essence. Cover and refrigerate until set, about 4 hours or overnight.

2. Form into tablespoon-sized balls and freeze for 10 minutes (see Techniques).

3. Temper the chocolate and dip each ball into it (see Techniques).

4. Store well sealed in the refrigerator or freezer.

OPTIONAL
GARNISHES

24 candied rose petals (page 112)
24 Royal Icing flowerets (page 111)

Chocolate Kahlúa Truffles

40 ONE-INCH
DIAMETER
TRUFFLES

These truffles can be flavored with either Kahlúa
or homemade coffee liqueur.

1 cup whipping cream
2 tablespoons unsalted butter
12 ounces bittersweet chocolate, very finely chopped
¼ cup Kahlúa or Coffee Liqueur (following recipe)

1¼ pounds bittersweet chocolate for dipping

1. In a heavy 1½- to 2-quart saucepan, scald the cream and butter.
   Remove from the heat and quickly stir in the chocolate until
   smooth. Cool 5 minutes, then add the Kahlúa or Coffee Liqueur. Cover and refrigerate until set, about 4 hours or
   overnight.

2. Form into tablespoon-sized balls and freeze for 10 minutes
   (see Techniques).

3. Temper the chocolate and dip each ball into it (see Techniques).

4. Store well sealed in the refrigerator or freezer.

OPTIONAL
GARNISHES

Decorate with threads of bittersweet chocolate (page
41)
40 mocha or chocolate coffee bean candies

Coffee Liqueur

1 QUART

Very easy and inexpensive to make. Make a double batch and give small bottles as gifts.

1¾ cups water
1½ cups sugar
1 vanilla bean
¾ cup freshly ground coffee
2 cups vodka

1. In a heavy 1½-quart saucepan, bring the water, sugar, and vanilla bean to a boil. Lower the heat and simmer for 10 minutes. Remove from the heat and add the coffee. Cool and add the vodka.

2. Age, unrefrigerated, but covered, 24 hours.

3. Strain through a double layer of cheesecloth. Bottle in sterilized brown glass bottles or jars (such as beer or stout bottles) and seal securely. Age in a cool place away from light for at least 2 weeks.

Chocolate Framboise Truffles

40 ONE-INCH DIAMETER TRUFFLES

Framboise is a syrup made from raspberries. It is available at gourmet and specialty food stores.

1 cup whipping cream
2 tablespoons framboise
14 ounces bittersweet chocolate, very finely chopped

1¼ pounds bittersweet chocolate for dipping

1. In a heavy 1½- to 2-quart saucepan, scald the cream and the framboise. (Framboise is so concentrated and heavy that it will separate out if not combined with the cream in this manner.) Remove from the heat and quickly stir in the chocolate until smooth. Cover and refrigerate until set, about 4 hours or overnight.

2. Form into tablespoon-sized balls and freeze for 10 minutes (see Techniques).

3. Temper the chocolate and dip each ball into it (see Techniques).

4. Store well sealed in the refrigerator or freezer.

OPTIONAL   40 red Royal Icing flowerets (page 111)
GARNISHES   40 raspberry candies, sometimes called pastilles
               (available at gourmet stores)

Chocolate Peanut Butter Truffles

36 ONE-INCH
DIAMETER
TRUFFLES

Similar to but a hundred times better than a popular candy that must herein go unnamed.

⅔ cup whipping cream
10 ounces bittersweet or milk chocolate, very finely chopped
½ cup natural peanut butter

....

1¼ pounds bittersweet or milk chocolate for dipping

1. In a heavy 1½- to 2-quart saucepan, scald the cream. Remove from the heat and quickly stir in the chocolate until smooth.

Fold in the peanut butter until smooth. Cover and refrigerate until set, about 4 hours or overnight.

2. Form into tablespoon-sized balls and freeze for 10 minutes (see Techniques).

3. Temper the chocolate and dip each ball into it (see Techniques).

4. Store well sealed in the refrigerator or freezer.

OPTIONAL   Decorate with threads of contrasting chocolate (page
GARNISHES   41)
                ½ cup chopped peanuts, sprinkled on top

Cinnamon Truffles

40 ONE-INCH
DIAMETER
TRUFFLES

Cinnamon and chocolate have been combined for millennia; the Aztec Indians added cinnamon to their chocolate drink. Use a mortar and pestle or an electric coffee grinder to grind cinnamon. These truffles are much better after aging 2 or 3 days.

1 cup whipping cream
10 ounces bittersweet chocolate, very finely chopped
3 tablespoons unsalted butter
2 tablespoons very strong black tea
2 teaspoons cinnamon, freshly ground

1¼ pounds chocolate for dipping

1. In a heavy 1½- to 2-quart saucepan, scald the cream. Remove from the heat and quickly stir in the chocolate until smooth.

Cool 5 minutes, then add the butter, tea, and cinnamon. Cover and refrigerate until set, about 4 hours or overnight.

2. Form into tablespoon-sized balls and freeze for 10 minutes (see Techniques).

3. Temper the chocolate and dip each ball into it (see Techniques).

4. Store well sealed in the refrigerator or freezer.

OPTIONAL   Threads of bittersweet chocolate (page 41)
GARNISHES   Roll in sweetened cocoa to which a pinch of cin-
                  namon has been added

Cranberry Cordial Truffles

45 ONE-INCH   A very interesting combination, somewhat tart and
DIAMETER   very fruity.
TRUFFLES

1 cup whipping cream
11 ounces bittersweet chocolate, very finely chopped
3 tablespoons unsalted butter
5 tablespoons Cranberry Jam (following recipe)
1 tablespoon kirschwasser or Grand Marnier

1¼ pounds bittersweet chocolate for dipping

1. In a heavy 1½- to 2-quart saucepan, scald the cream. Remove from the heat and quickly stir in the chocolate until smooth. Cool 5 minutes, then add the butter, jam, and liqueur. Cover and refrigerate until set, about 4 hours or overnight.

2. Form into tablespoon-sized balls and freeze for 10 minutes (see Techniques).

3. Temper the chocolate and dip each ball into it (see Techniques).

4. Store well sealed in the refrigerator or freezer.

VARIATIONS   Use strawberry, raspberry, or blackberry jam instead
                  of the cranberry jam.

OPTIONAL   45 red Royal Icing flowerets (page 111)
GARNISHES   Threads of white chocolate (page 41)

Cranberry or Other Berry Jam

This recipe for jam is a simple formula, one part
fruit to one part sugar, and is very easy to make.

*Fruit (cranberries, strawberries, raspberries, or
    blackberries)*
Sugar
Lemon juice if necessary

1. Place an equal amount by volume of rinsed and crushed fruit
   and sugar in a heavy saucepan at least 6 times larger than the
   cold volume of the uncooked jam. If the fruit is very ripe, add 1
   tablespoon of lemon juice per pound of fruit. Bring to a boil,
   stirring constantly. Turn the heat down to a simmer and cook
   until a small amount "sets" on a spoon after 5 minutes in the
   refrigerator. For 1 cup fruit and 1 cup sugar, about 20 minutes
   is the proper cooking time.

2. Ladle into clean jars and store refrigerated or frozen.

3. Before adding to a ganache, put the jam in a strainer and allow to drain about 10 minutes. Make the ganache with the thick part remaining in the strainer.

Chestnut and Kirsch Truffles

40 ONE-INCH
DIAMETER
TRUFFLES

Chestnut spread is available canned at specialty stores. These are a delightful midwinter treat.

1 cup whipping cream
1 pound bittersweet chocolate, very finely chopped
1/4 cup kirschwasser
1 cup sweetened chestnut spread (250 grams or 8 3/4-ounce can)

1 to 1 1/4 pounds bittersweet chocolate for dipping

1. In a heavy 1½- to 2-quart saucepan, scald the cream. Remove from the heat and quickly stir in the chocolate until completely melted. Blend in the kirschwasser then the chestnut spread.

2. Cover and refrigerate until set, about 4 hours or overnight.

3. Form into tablespoon-sized balls and freeze for 10 minutes (see Techniques).

4. Temper the chocolate and dip each ball into it (see Techniques).

5. Store well sealed in the refrigerator or freezer.

OPTIONAL
GARNISH

Threads of bittersweet chocolate (page 41)

Sour Cream Truffles

25 ONE-INCH
DIAMETER
TRUFFLES

Truffles can be made with sour as well as whipping cream.

8 ounces bittersweet chocolate, very finely chopped
⅔ cup sour cream
2 tablespoons unsalted butter

1¼ pounds bittersweet chocolate for dipping

1. In the top of a double boiler, over hot but not simmering water, melt the chocolate in the sour cream. Remove from the heat and stir in the butter. Cover and refrigerate until set, about 4 hours or overnight.

2. Form into tablespoon-sized balls and freeze for 10 minutes (see Techniques).

3. Temper the chocolate and dip each ball into it (see Techniques).

4. Store well sealed in the refrigerator or freezer.

OPTIONAL
GARNISHES

Threads of white chocolate (page 41)
Dip half in white chocolate for a harlequin effect (page 41)

UNDIPPED
TRUFFLES

Roasted Almond Balls

40 THREE-QUARTER-INCH DIAMETER TRUFFLES

Crunchy with almonds inside and out, these truffles are very easy to make.

1 cup whipping cream
11 ounces bittersweet chocolate, very finely chopped
2 tablespoons unsalted butter
3 tablespoons strong coffee, water, or liqueur
1 cup (4 ounces) unblanched almonds, roasted and finely chopped

1 cup (4 ounces) unblanched almonds, roasted and finely chopped

1. In a heavy 1½- to 2-quart saucepan, scald the cream. Quickly stir in the chocolate. Cool 5 minutes, then add the butter, almonds, and coffee, water, or liqueur. Cover and refrigerate until set, about 4 hours or overnight.

2. Form into tablespoon-sized balls (see Techniques). Roll each ball in the remaining 1 cup roasted almonds.

3. Store well sealed in the refrigerator or freezer.

VARIATIONS   Substitute Brazil nuts, cashews, macadamia nuts, or pecans for the almonds.

OPTIONAL GARNISH   Roll in sweetened or unsweetened cocoa

Chocolate Apricot Balls

40 THREE-
QUARTER-INCH
DIAMETER
TRUFFLES

These undipped truffles are reminiscent of the famous Sacher Torte, which features chocolate,
apricot jam, and kirschwasser.

1 cup whipping cream
11 ounces bittersweet chocolate, very finely chopped
2 tablespoons unsalted butter
¾ cup (4 ounces) dried apricots, finely chopped
3 tablespoons kirschwasser or triple sec liqueur

Cocoa, sweetened or unsweetened, for rolling

1. In a heavy 1½- to 2-quart saucepan, scald the cream. Quickly
   stir in the chocolate. Cool 5 minutes, then add the butter, apricots, and liqueur. Cover and refrigerate until set, about 4 hours
   or overnight.

2. Form into tablespoon-sized balls and roll in cocoa (see
   Techniques).

3. Store well sealed in the refrigerator or freezer.

VARIATIONS   Substitute dried figs, papaya, or prunes for the
                 apricots.

Milk Chocolate Truffles

24 THREE-
QUARTER-INCH
DIAMETER
TRUFFLES

Great for children (or adults) who prefer a sweet, milky taste.

8 ounces milk chocolate, very finely chopped
2 tablespoons unsalted butter
¼ cup whipping cream

Sweetened cocoa powder

1. In the top of a double boiler, over hot but not simmering water, melt the chocolate, butter, and cream. Cover and refrigerate until set, about 4 hours or overnight.

2. Form into tablespoon-sized balls and roll in cocoa (see Techniques).

3. Store well sealed in the refrigerator or freezer.

Bourbon Balls

45 THREE-
QUARTER-INCH
DIAMETER
TRUFFLES

Make these truffles several days ahead so the flavors can mellow and marry.

12 ounces bittersweet chocolate, very finely chopped
⅔ cup unsalted butter
4 egg yolks (about ¼ cup), lightly beaten
⅓ cup bourbon

Cocoa, sweetened or unsweetened, for rolling

1. In the top of a double boiler, over hot but not simmering water, melt the chocolate and butter. Remove from the heat. Cool 5 minutes and add the egg yolks and bourbon. Cover and refrigerate until set, about 4 hours or overnight.

2. Form into tablespoon-sized balls and roll each ball in cocoa (see Techniques).

3. Store well sealed in the refrigerator or freezer.

VARIATIONS   Substitute rum, whiskey, Scotch, or Drambuie for the bourbon.

Hazelnut Cream Truffles

40 THREE-
QUARTER-INCH
DIAMETER
TRUFFLES

Chocolate and ground hazelnuts are a popular combination in France. Do not attempt to shortcut this recipe by not roasting the hazelnuts; their flavor and texture are much improved after roasting.

*7 ounces hazelnuts or ⅔ cup hazelnut paste
    (available at gourmet stores)
1 cup whipping cream
14 ounces bittersweet chocolate, very finely chopped
2 tablespoons Frangelico (hazelnut liqueur) or
    coffee*

Cocoa, sweetened or unsweetened, for rolling

1. Roast the hazelnuts under a broiler until the skins are very dark, almost black. Shake the baking sheet a few times while the nuts are roasting to assure that they brown evenly. Cool and

rub the nuts together in your hands to remove the skins. Re-roast any nuts that are difficult to skin. (This process is tedious but necessary.) In a blender or food processor, grind the nuts until smooth and semiliquid. Measure ⅔ cup.

2. In a heavy 1½- to 2-quart saucepan, scald the cream. Remove from the heat and quickly stir in the chocolate until smooth. Cool 5 minutes, then add the ground hazelnuts and liquid. Cover and refrigerate until set, about 4 hours or overnight.

3. Form into tablespoon-sized balls and roll in cocoa (see Techniques).

4. Store well sealed in the refrigerator or freezer.

Creamy Chocolate Mints

36 ONE-INCH
SQUARE
MINTS

Extremely easy and delicious. Impress your guests with these simple-to-make after-dinner mints.

⅔ cup whipping cream
12 ounces bittersweet chocolate, very finely chopped
¼ teaspoon peppermint extract (not oil)

Cocoa, sweetened or unsweetened, for rolling

1. In a heavy 1½- to 2-quart saucepan, scald the cream. Remove from the heat and quickly stir in the chocolate until completely melted. Cool 5 minutes, then add the mint extract.

2. Pour into a loaf pan 4 by 9 inches or on a marble slab with candy rails set 4 by 9 inches. Cover and refrigerate until set, about 4 hours or overnight.

3. Cut into 1-inch squares (getting the first one out of your loaf pan intact may be tricky). Tease back into square shapes if necessary.

4. Roll each square in cocoa. Store well sealed in the refrigerator or freezer.

COOKED
SUGAR-BASED
CHOCOLATE
CONFECTIONS

Chocolate-covered Caramels

These chewy, delicious caramels are easy to make, but you must use unhomogenized and preferably raw (unpasteurized) milk. The stabilizers in homogenized milk cause the solids in the milk to coagulate, sink to the bottom, and burn! Look for unhomogenized, raw milk at any health food store.

1½ cups raw milk
2½ cups sugar
½ cup mildly flavored honey
½ cup unsalted butter
1 inch vanilla bean or ½ teaspoon vanilla extract

....

1½ pounds bittersweet chocolate for dipping

1. Butter a 12-by-12-inch piece of marble with candy rails set 8 by 8 inches, or a baking sheet. Also, butter a cleaver or French knife.

2. In a heavy 5-quart saucepan, heat the milk gradually, then add all other ingredients (except the vanilla extract if you are using it). Bring to a boil, stirring constantly. Clip on a thermometer and cook the mixture to 248°F., stirring gently (about 15 minutes).

3. Remove from the heat. Remove the vanilla bean or add the vanilla extract. Cool 2 minutes while stirring, then pour onto the marble slab or baking sheet. If you do not have rails and your sheet is not 8 by 8 inches, tease the caramel into an 8-by-8-inch square by folding it back on itself until it is the proper size and is cool enough to keep its shape. Cool 10

minutes, then score into 1-inch cubes. If you cannot dip each piece right away, wrap each piece individually in a piece of wax paper 4 by 5 inches and twist the ends of the paper tightly. If the caramel is not completely cool, it will melt the wax and the paper will be stuck to it forever.

4. Temper the chocolate and dip each cube into it (see Techniques).

5. Store well sealed in the refrigerator. Do not freeze.

OPTIONAL
GARNISH

Roll each cube in unsweetened cocoa powder

Chocolate Caramels

48 ROLLS
2½ INCHES
LONG AND
½ INCH IN
DIAMETER

Similar but much better than a very popular rolled chocolate confection.

¾ cup raw milk
1 cup sugar
⅓ cup mildly flavored honey
¼ cup unsalted butter
6 ounces bittersweet chocolate, very finely chopped

1. Butter a 12-inch-square marble slab with candy rails set at 8 by 8 inches, or a baking sheet. Also, butter a French knife or cleaver.

2. In a heavy 4-quart saucepan, heat the milk gradually, then add the sugar, honey, and butter. Bring to a boil, stirring constantly. Clip on a thermometer and cook to 248°F., stirring gently (about 10 minutes). Remove from the heat and stir in the chocolate. Continue stirring for 2 minutes.

3. Pour onto the marble or baking sheet. If you have no rails, tease the caramel into an 8-by-8-inch square by folding it back on itself until it is cool enough to keep its shape. Cool 10 minutes and then cut into approximately 2½-inch by ½-inch rectangles with the knife. It may be necessary to rebutter the knife.

4. Roll each piece in wax paper cut 3 by 5 inches, and twist the ends tightly. If the caramel is not completely cool it will melt the wax, causing the paper to stick to it forever.

5. Store unrefrigerated, but in a cool place, well sealed from light and moisture. Do not freeze.

Chocolate-covered Fondant

1¼ POUNDS
OR 40 THREE-
QUARTER-INCH
DIAMETER
CENTERS

Fondant is a very smooth and creamy paste made simply of sugar and water. It is used in marzipan, chocolate-dipped cherries, or can be molded, flavored, and dipped. Fondant needs an aging or ripening period of at least 48 hours, so plan ahead. As fondant keeps for at least 6 months, it is a good idea to make a double batch and keep it on hand.

⅔ cup water
2 cups sugar
2 tablespoons light corn syrup

1¼ pounds bittersweet chocolate for dipping

1. Set candy rails 10 by 10 inches on a marble slab or have a rimmed baking sheet or platter ready.

2. In a heavy 2-quart saucepan, place the water, sugar, and corn syrup. Bring to a boil. Turn off the heat and cover for 5 minutes. Wipe away any undissolved sugar crystals on the sides of the pan with a damp paper towel or napkin wrapped around a fork. *Be very thorough; one crystal could ruin the entire batch.* Clip on a thermometer and cook without stirring to 238°F.

3. Remove from heat and pour onto the marble slab or baking sheet *without scraping the pan*, to avoid picking up crystals. Cool to 110°F., or until the marble slab or baking sheet is cool enough to touch.

4. With fondant paddles or plastic or metal scrapers, fold and turn the syrup over on itself. After a few minutes, the syrup will start to stiffen and turn cloudy and white. Continue working the syrup until it loses its shine, is stiff enough to form a ball, and seems dry.

5. Put in a bowl and cover with plastic or place in a plastic bag. Age at least 48 hours in the refrigerator or other cool place.

6. Place the fondant in the top of a double boiler over simmering water. Add any flavoring and coloring desired. Melt the fondant and blend in the flavor and color if any. Allow to dry out 5 minutes over the simmering water.

7. Form into tablespoon-sized balls and place on wax or parchment paper.

8. Temper the chocolate and dip each ball into it (see Techniques).

9. Store unrefrigerated, but in a cool place, well sealed from light and moisture. Do not freeze.

VARIATIONS   Add to the ripened fondant before melting:

⅛ teaspoon peppermint oil or extract
1 drop red food color

¼ teaspoon rose essence
1 drop red food color

⅛ teaspoon spearmint oil or extract
2 drops green food color

¼ teaspoon lemon oil or extract
2 drops yellow food color

¼ teaspoon orange oil or extract
2 drops yellow and 1 drop red food color

OPTIONAL   40 appropriately colored Royal Icing flowerets (page
GARNISH   111)

Cocoa Fudge

32 ONE-INCH   Relatively inexpensive to make, this is nonetheless
CUBES   rich and creamy.

2 cups sugar, preferably vanilla sugar
¼ cup light corn syrup
⅔ cup cocoa powder
¾ cup milk or half and half
⅓ cup unsalted butter
½ teaspoon vanilla extract (omit if vanilla sugar used)

1. Butter an 8-by-4-inch loaf pan.

2. In a heavy 3-quart saucepan, place all ingredients except the butter and vanilla extract. Bring to a boil, stirring constantly. Clip on a thermometer and cook until the mixture reaches

238°F., stirring occasionally. Remove from the heat and cool to 110°F. without stirring.

3. Add the butter and extract and beat until mixture loses its gloss and becomes thick. Pour into the prepared pan and refrigerate until set, about 30 minutes. Cut into 1-inch cubes.

4. Store unrefrigerated, but in a cool place, well sealed from light and moisture.

Chocolate Fudge

32 ONE-INCH
CUBES

Velvety smooth and sweet.

2 cups sugar, preferably vanilla sugar
1 cup milk or half and half
6 ounces bittersweet chocolate, very finely chopped
2 tablespoons light corn syrup
2 tablespoons unsalted butter
1/2 teaspoon vanilla extract (omit if vanilla sugar used)

Follow the procedures for Cocoa Fudge, preceding recipe.

Chocolate Fudge II

32 ONE-INCH
CUBES

This fudge is made with unsweetened chocolate.

2 cups sugar, preferably vanilla sugar
1/4 cup light corn syrup

> 4 ounces unsweetened chocolate, very finely
>   chopped
> 1 cup milk or half and half
> 1/4 cup unsalted butter
> 1/2 teaspoon vanilla extract (omit if vanilla sugar is
>   used)

Follow the procedures for Cocoa Fudge.

Mexican Chocolate Fudge

32 ONE-INCH
CUBES

Chocolate from Mexico has a distinctive flavor and aroma. It is more earthy and sweeter than European-made chocolate. The Ibarra brand from Guadalajara, packaged in an octagonal bright yellow and red box, is widely available in the United States at gourmet stores.

> 3 tablets Mexican chocolate (10 ounces)
> 1 cup milk or half and half
> 1 1/2 cups sugar, preferably vanilla sugar
> 1/4 cup light corn syrup
> 1/4 cup unsalted butter
> 1/4 teaspoon ground cinnamon

Follow the procedures for Cocoa Fudge.

Chocolate-covered Marshmallows

45 ONE-INCH
CUBES

If the only marshmallows you've ever eaten are the tasteless dead air sold in supermarkets, you are in for a delightful surprise. Incomparably better, these are fluffy and tender on the inside and only slightly firm on the outside. These marshmallows are inexpensive and easy to make if you have a heavy duty mixer. Marshmallows are most successfully made when there is little humidity.

¼ cup powdered sugar
2 tablespoons cornstarch

1 tablespoon granulated unflavored gelatin
¼ cup cold water
⅓ cup light corn syrup
1 cup sugar
¼ cup warm water

1 pound milk chocolate or bittersweet chocolate for dipping

1. Sift the powdered sugar and cornstarch together. Sprinkle half the mixture into a loaf pan 5 by 9 inches; set aside.

2. In the bowl of a mixing machine, place the gelatin and cold water. Let sit 5 minutes or until firm and grainy-looking (this will happen while you cook the syrup in the following step).

3. In a heavy 1½- to 2-quart saucepan, cook the corn syrup, sugar, and warm water to 246°F. Remove from the heat and pour over

the gelatin. Stir until dissolved and then beat 12 to 15 minutes at a high speed. Use a timer; underbeaten mallow has a texture like white glue.

4. Fold into the prepared pan and level with a palette knife. Sprinkle with the remaining sugar/cornstarch mixture and cover with plastic wrap. Refrigerate until set, about 1 hour.

5. Place scissors in the freezer for 10 minutes. Loosen the edges of the mallow by running a knife along the sides of the pan, if necessary. Turn the entire mass out on a rack. Do not throw away the sugar/cornstarch mixture. Rub the blades of the scissors with it and snip the mass into 1-inch cubes. Roll the cut, sticky edges in the remaining sugar/cornstarch. Dry on a rack until stiff, about 1 hour.

6. Dust off any excess sugar/cornstarch. Temper the chocolate and dip each marshmallow into it (see Techniques). Place on wax or parchment paper to set.

7. Store unrefrigerated, but in a cool place, well sealed from light and moisture. Do not freeze.

VARIATIONS   Add ½ teaspoon rose essence and 3 drops of red food color to the gelatin before pouring in the syrup.

Add ¼ teaspoon peppermint extract and 6 drops of green food color to the gelatin before pouring in the syrup.

Fold in 2 ounces very finely ground bittersweet chocolate to the cooked syrup.

Add ¼ cup unsweetened cocoa to the corn syrup, sugar, and water mixture before it cooks.

OPTIONAL   35 appropriately colored Royal Icing flowerets (page
GARNISH   111)

Chocolate Peanut Brittle

50 ONE-INCH
SQUARE
PIECES

An inexpensive but popular candy. Do not attempt to make a double batch; it cools very quickly and a large batch would cool before you could spread it thin enough.

1 cup sugar
½ cup corn syrup
¼ teaspoon salt
¼ cup water
1 tablespoon unsalted butter
¾ cup whole peanuts, roasted but not salted (if necessary, blanch them in water to remove salt and dry well)
3 ounces bittersweet chocolate, very finely chopped

1. Butter a 12-by-12-inch marble slab or baking sheet.

2. In a heavy 3-quart saucepan, place the sugar, corn syrup, salt, and water. Bring to a boil while stirring constantly. Clip on a thermometer and cook to 252°F. without stirring.

3. Add the butter and peanuts and cook to 300°F., gently stirring.

4. Remove from the heat and stir in the chocolate.

5. *Immediately* pour onto the marble or baking sheet. As the syrup hardens within 10 seconds, pour in a spiral rather than in one big puddle; otherwise the syrup may harden before it settles completely and be very thick in the center. Spread as thin as possible with a palette knife into a square at least 7 by 7 inches. Quickly score the candy into 1-inch squares with a cleaver or French knife.

6. Store unrefrigerated, but in a cool place, well sealed from light and moisture. Do not freeze.

Chocolate-covered Toffee

Crunchy, buttery, and sweet.

2 cups sugar
¼ cup light corn syrup
½ cup evaporated milk or half and half
½ cup unsalted butter
⅛ teaspoon salt

1¼ pounds bittersweet chocolate for dipping

1. Butter a 12-by-12-inch marble slab or baking sheet. If you have them, set candy rails 7 by 8 inches.

2. In a heavy 3-quart saucepan, place all ingredients except chocolate. Bring to a boil, stirring constantly. Clip on a thermometer and cook to 280°F., stirring gently. (Do not stir so vigorously that the cooking mixture does not bubble.)

3. Pour onto the marble or baking sheet. If you do not have candy rails, when slightly cool, tease with a palette knife into a 7-by-8-inch rectangle ¼ inch thick. Score into 1-inch squares halfway through when the toffee is sufficiently cooled. When completely cooled, snap into pieces.

4. Temper the chocolate and dip each square into it (see Techniques).

5. Store unrefrigerated, but in a cool place, well sealed from light and moisture. Do not freeze.

OPTIONAL
GARNISH   Threads of bittersweet chocolate (page 41).

Chocolate-dipped Torrone

64 ONE-INCH
CUBES

In the United States, a variation of this confection is called sea foam or divinity, in France, nougat, but this Swiss version is the tastiest.

½ cup sugar
2 tablespoons water
½ cup honey

⅓ cup egg whites (from 2 to 3 large eggs)

1⅓ cups light corn syrup
1⅓ cups sugar

3 tablespoons unsalted butter, cubed
1½ cups nuts (almonds, hazelnuts, and/or pistachio
  nuts), chopped
½ cup candied cherries, chopped

1¼ pounds bittersweet chocolate for dipping

1. Butter an 8-by-8-inch pan, or line it with wafer paper (available at Chinese groceries).

2. In a heavy 2-quart saucepan, place ½ cup sugar, the water, and honey. Bring to a boil. Turn off the heat and cover for 5 minutes. Wipe away any undissolved sugar crystals on the sides of the pan with a damp paper towel wrapped around a fork. *Be very thorough; one crystal could ruin the entire batch.* Clip on a thermometer and cook without stirring to 238°F. Remove from the heat.

3. Beat the egg whites until very stiff. Slowly pour the hot syrup onto the beaten egg whites. Continue to beat for 5 minutes. The mass will get very thick.

4. In the same heavy 2-quart saucepan you used for the first syrup, place the light corn syrup and 1⅓ cups sugar. Bring to a boil while stirring. Clip on a thermometer and cook without stirring to 285°F. Remove from the heat and pour into the first mass and beat until well mixed. Add the butter, nuts, and candied cherries.

5. Pour into the prepared pan. Set in a cool, dry place for 24 hours. Invert onto a baking sheet or marble slab. Cut into 1-inch cubes.

6. Temper the chocolate and dip each cube into it (see Techniques).

7. Store unrefrigerated, but in a cool place, well sealed from light and moisture. Do not freeze.

OTHER
CHOCOLATE
CONFECTIONS

Turtles

MAKES 30

Similar in flavor to elegant European Florentines, this American version of the nut, caramel, and chocolate confection resembles its namesake.

120 walnut or pecan halves (about 1/2 pound)
1/2 caramel recipe (page 77)
6 ounces bittersweet or milk chocolate, very finely chopped
2 tablespoons unsalted butter

1. Arrange the nuts in groups of 4 on wax or parchment paper. Sort the nuts so that similar-sized ones are grouped together. Butter a marble slab or baking sheet.

2. Make the caramel. Pour it out onto the marble or baking sheet. Cool 1 minute, or until cool enough to handle. Pinch off a generous teaspoon-sized amount of the caramel and press it into the middle of a nut group. Tease the nut group back into the correct form if necessary. Repeat with remainder of caramel and nuts.

3. In the top of a double boiler over hot but not simmering water, melt the chocolate and butter. Spoon scant teaspoon-sized amounts onto the caramels.

4. When the chocolate has set, store in a cool place, well sealed from light and moisture. Do not freeze.

Chocolate Nut Bark

1 POUND, OR
36 ONE-AND-
A-HALF-INCH
SQUARE
PIECES

Extremely simple to make. You will never buy overpriced nut bark again.

1 1/2 cups whole nuts, blanched or unblanched
(almonds, cashews, Brazil nuts, macadamia nuts,
pecans, or walnuts)
12 ounces bittersweet or milk chocolate, very finely
chopped

1. Arrange the nuts on a piece of wax or parchment paper 9 by 9 inches.

2. Temper the chocolate and spread it over the nuts with a palette knife. Allow to set, then score into 1½-inch square pieces with a cleaver or French knife.

3. Store in a cool place, well sealed from light and moisture. Do not freeze.

Rocky Road

1½ POUNDS,
OR
36 ONE-AND-
A-HALF-INCH
CUBES

The contrast of textures is what makes this confection interesting: the crunchy nuts, the fluffy marshmallows, and the smooth chocolate.

1 1/2 cups marshmallows (page 84) cut into 1/4-inch
cubes or purchased miniature marshmallows
4 ounces unblanched almonds, coarsely chopped
1 pound bittersweet or milk chocolate, very finely
chopped

1. Line a baking sheet or flat platter at least 9 inches square with wax or parchment paper. Sprinkle the marshmallows and nuts evenly on the paper.

2. Temper the chocolate (see Techniques) and spread it over the marshmallows and nuts. Allow the chocolate to set and then with a knife cut into pieces 1½ inches square.

3. Store unrefrigerated, but in a cool place, well sealed from light and moisture.

Molded Chocolate Candy Box

MAKES 1
SIX-INCH
ROUND BOX
HOLDING
6 TO 7
TRUFFLES

This box makes an entirely edible gift, as the recipient can eat it as well as the goodies inside. It is rather time-consuming to make if you don't have a special mold, but very beautiful. Use a "virgin" cake pan as any scratches will show and mar your creation.

1 pound bittersweet or white chocolate (the box will weigh only 10 ounces but the extra chocolate is necessary for tempering)

1. Rub a 6-inch round cake pan with a bland vegetable oil.

2. Temper the chocolate. Pour a ladleful of chocolate into the pan. Tilt and rock the pan back and forth until the chocolate is spread evenly over the bottom. Refrigerate 15 minutes. Pour another ladleful of chocolate into the pan and ease it onto the sides by rolling the pan and then using a palette knife. Refrigerate 15 minutes. If the side is not thick enough (⅛ inch is the appropriate thickness), add another ladleful of chocolate and repeat the shaping process, otherwise invert; the box should

pull away from the pan. Refrigerate another 15 minutes and trim the edges with a serrated knife.

3. Repeat Step 2 to make the top of the box, but don't make the sides quite as high.

4. Decorate by piping designs from a pastry bag in a contrasting color of chocolate or with Royal Icing flowerets (page 111).

5. Store in a cool place, well sealed from light and moisture. Do not freeze.

Chocolate-covered Cherries

40 TO 50 CONFECTIONS

These dainties require advance planning (at least a month from start to finish) but they are worth it. Warn your guests that there are pits in the cherries. If you want the centers to be liquidy, use the glycerine and acetic acid; they make the fondant liquefy after sitting an hour. Glycerine and acetic acid can be purchased at pharmacies.

1 cup sugar
1 cup water
1 cup brandy or kirschwasser

1 pound fresh cherries

2 pounds fondant (page 79)
2 drops glycerine (optional)
2 drops 36 percent acetic acid (optional)

1½ pounds bittersweet chocolate for dipping

1. In a heavy saucepan, bring the sugar and water to a boil; cook 5 minutes. Cool and add the brandy or kirschwasser.

2. Rinse the cherries. Do not stem or pit them. Place the cherries in a clean quart jar and pour the syrup over them. Seal and refrigerate at least 1 month and up to 6 months.

3. Drain the syrup from the cherries. In the top of a double boiler over simmering water, melt the fondant (with the glycerine and acetic acid, if desired, for a liquidy center). Dip each cherry in the mixture and place on wax or parchment paper to set.

4. Temper the chocolate and dip each cherry into it (see Techniques).

5. If you used the glycerine and acetic acid, wrap each cherry in confectioners' foil because the liquid from the center may seep out; otherwise store refrigerated and well sealed. Do not freeze.

Some-More Truffles

32 ONE-AND-A-QUARTER-INCH DIAMETER TRUFFLES

An improvement on a delightful memory from childhood, this is a variation on what every Girl Scout makes on every camping trip. These all-American treats look surprisingly elegant, like miniature Doboshtortes.

4 cups marshmallows, or 2 cups marshmallow
  cream or unset marshmallow (recipe page 84)
16 graham crackers (2 by 4 inches)
1 pound bittersweet or milk chocolate for dipping

1. In the top of a double boiler, over simmering water, melt the marshmallows. Spread a thin layer over a graham cracker, sandwich another graham cracker on the marshmallow cream and repeat the process until you have a club sandwich of 4 graham crackers and 3 layers of marshmallow. Be careful to align the crackers precisely.

2. Freeze the sandwiches half an hour. With a narrow-bladed serrated knife or cheese cutting wire, cut the frozen sandwiches in 8 cubes (1 cut lengthwise and 3 cuts widthwise). Brush away any crumbs (if the crackers were properly aligned, there should be very few).

3. Temper the chocolate and dip each cube into it (see Techniques).

4. Store unrefrigerated but in a cool place, well sealed from light and moisture. These truffles are suitable for freezing.

OPTIONAL   32 whole unblanched almonds
GARNISHES   32 Royal Icing flowerets (page 111)

Brownie Truffles

48 ONE-INCH
DIAMETER
TRUFFLES

If you love brownies, and what chocolate lover doesn't, you'll love these truffles made from brownies formed into balls and then dipped. This recipe for brownies first appeared in my *Ultimate Chocolate Cake Book*.

7 ounces bittersweet chocolate, very finely chopped
6 tablespoons (3 ounces) unsalted butter, very soft
3 large (¾ cup) eggs

¾ cup (6 ounces) sugar
¾ cup sifted and then measured (3 ounces) all-
purpose flour

....

1¼ pounds bittersweet chocolate for dipping

1. Preheat oven to 350°F. Butter a 9-by-12-inch baking pan. Line it with wax paper, then butter and flour the paper.

2. In the top of a double boiler, over hot water, melt the chocolate and butter; set aside. Beat the eggs with the sugar until very creamy, about 2 minutes. Alternately, a third at a time, fold the chocolate and the flour into the egg mixture.

3. Pour into the prepared pan and bake until a knife inserted into the center comes out clean, about 25 minutes.

4. When half cooled, cut into 48 1½-inch squares and roll into balls. Freeze 30 minutes and brush away any crumbs.

5. Temper the chocolate and dip each ball into it (see Techniques).

6. Store in a cool place, well sealed from light and moisture. These truffles are suitable for freezing.

Peanut Butter and Cream Cheese Truffles

....
40 ONE-INCH
DIAMETER
TRUFFLES

Remember that candy is not just for adults. Children love peanut butter in almost any form, but especially with chocolate. Make these for a child's birthday or holiday party.

12 ounces cream cheese
1 cup crunchy natural peanut butter
3 cups sifted and then measured (12 ounces)
  confectioners' sugar

....

1¼ pounds bittersweet or milk chocolate for dipping

1. Combine the cream cheese, peanut butter, and sugar. This is most easily done by softening the cream cheese and peanut butter in a double boiler and stirring in the sugar. Cover and refrigerate until set, 4 hours or overnight.

2. Form into tablespoon-sized balls and freeze for 10 minutes (see Techniques).

3. Temper the chocolate and dip each ball into it (see Techniques).

4. Store well sealed in the refrigerator or freezer.

OPTIONAL   ½ cup chopped peanuts sprinkled on top
GARNISHES   40 Royal Icing flowerets (page 111)

Coconut Macaroon Truffles

....
30 ONE-INCH
DIAMETER
TRUFFLES

Solid coconut on the inside, these are moist, chewy, and delicious.

4 ounces unsweetened, dried coconut (2 cups not
  packed)
½ cup sugar
⅓ cup egg whites (from 2 to 3 large eggs), lightly
  beaten

....

2 tablespoons rum (optional)
1 pound bittersweet chocolate for dipping

1. Preheat the oven to 350°F. Butter a baking sheet or line it with wax or parchment paper.

2. Mix the coconut and sugar. Add the egg whites and blend until smooth. Form into ¾-inch diameter balls and place 1 inch apart on the baking sheet. Bake until slightly golden brown, about 25 minutes. While still slightly warm, re-form any balls that lost their round shape while baking.

3. Sprinkle the rum over the balls, if desired.

4. Temper the chocolate and dip each ball into it (see Techniques).

5. Store unrefrigerated but in a cool place, well sealed from light and moisture. These truffles are suitable for freezing.

OPTIONAL
GARNISHES
Threads of white chocolate (page 41)
¼ cup coconut, sprinkled on top

Chocolate-dipped Strawberries

40 BERRIES

The juicy, soft berry contrasts beautifully with the brittle chocolate. The chocolate enhances the aroma and flavor of the berry, making it seem more intense. These confections do not keep very long and must be served within 6 hours.

4 pint baskets strawberries
1 to 1¼ pounds bittersweet chocolate for dipping

1. Wipe the strawberries off with a dry cloth. Do not wash or rinse them lest the moisture contaminate the dipping chocolate.

2. Temper the chocolate (see Techniques). Holding each berry by the stem or with a toothpick or cake tester, dip into the chocolate and allow the excess to drain before placing it on wax or parchment paper to set.

3. Store at a very cool room temperature or refrigerated only up to 6 hours before serving.

Chocolate-dipped
Strawberries Trianon

These make an extremely elegant, even dazzling dessert.

4 berries and 1 to 2 ounces of chocolate per serving

1. Wipe the strawberries off with a dry cloth; do not wash or rinse them lest the moisture contaminate the dipping chocolate. Arrange the berries on wax or parchment paper in groups of 4, 3 for the base and 1 for the top. The base berries should be of similar size and the top berry should be slightly smaller. Set the top berries aside (do not dip).

2. Temper the chocolate (see Techniques) and dip each berry into it. Allow the excess to drip off before placing the berries back together on paper in their groups of 3, pressing them together as tightly as possible. With a pastry brush or chopstick, add a little more chocolate to the intersections of the berries to cement them together securely. Place a dab of choc-

olate in the center of each berry group and place the top berry on it. After the chocolate dab has set, ladle more over the top berry, making sure it is completely covered.

3. Store as for Chocolate-dipped Strawberries (preceding recipe).

OPTIONAL   Thread with white or bittersweet chocolate (page 41)
GARNISH

Truffle or Dipped Strawberry "Croquembouche"

50 TO 75
SERVINGS
FOR THE
STRAWBERRY
MOUNTAIN

This tour de force resembles the pastry mountain made with miniature creampuffs. It is a lot of work, but a spectacular and scrumptious centerpiece for a party. This is the one instance when you want your truffles to have a "foot." The foot rests on the side of the form.

75 TO 150
SERVINGS
FOR THE
TRUFFLE
MOUNTAIN

1 pound bittersweet chocolate for glue
150 dipped truffles (a variety of white, bittersweet,
*   and milk chocolate-dipped looks the best) or 150*
*   Chocolate-dipped Strawberries (see recipe)*

1. Make the cardboard form as per the diagram. Cover the form with foil. Place the form on a serving platter.

2. Temper the chocolate (see Techniques).

3. Starting at the base, place a row of truffles or berries against the form. Dab a little tempered chocolate between them as glue. Build up, one row at a time, pressing the foot of the

truffle or berry against the side of the form and using tempered chocolate as glue. If you are using truffles dipped in different kinds of chocolate, make a pattern of the colors.

4. Thread the constructed mountain with the leftover chocolate if desired (page 41).

Uncooked Chocolate-covered Marshmallows

32 ONE-INCH CUBES

The initial time necessary to make this recipe is less than for the cooked marshmallows but they do not set as fast nor keep so well.

¼ cup powdered sugar
2 tablespoons cornstarch

2 teaspoons granulated unflavored gelatin
¼ cup cold water
⅓ cup sugar
⅓ cup light corn syrup

....

1 pound milk or bittersweet chocolate for dipping

1. Sift the powdered sugar and cornstarch together. Sprinkle half the mixture into a loaf pan 4 by 8 inches. Set aside.

2. Place the gelatin in the top of a double boiler. Add the water and let set five minutes or until firm and grainy-looking. Turn on the heat and melt the gelatin. Stir in the sugar and corn syrup. Transfer to a bowl of a mixing machine and beat at a high speed for 15 minutes (use a timer).

3. Fold into the prepared pan and level with a palette knife. Sprinkle with the remaining sugar/cornstarch mixture and cover with plastic wrap. Refrigerate until set, at least 4 hours or overnight.

4. Place scissors in the freezer for 10 minutes. Loosen the edges of the mallow by running a knife along the sides of the pan if necessary. Turn the entire mass out on a rack, reserving the sugar/cornstarch. Rub the blades of the scissors with it. Snip the mass into 1-inch cubes. Roll the sticky cut edges into the remaining sugar/cornstarch. Dry, unrefrigerated, at least 4 hours or overnight, covered.

5. Dust off any excess sugar/cornstarch. Temper the chocolate and dip each marshmallow in it (see Techniques).

6. Store unrefrigerated, but in a cool place, well sealed from light and moisture.

OPTIONAL   30 appropriately colored Royal Icing flowerets (page
GARNISH   111)

Chocolate-covered Marzipan

32 ONE-INCH
DIAMETER
TRUFFLES

The recipe for marzipan is simply one part nuts to one part fondant by weight. Marzipan is usually made with blanched almonds, but can also be made with walnuts.

8 ounces blanched almonds or walnuts
8 ounces fondant (page 79)
½ teaspoon vanilla extract, orange flower water, or kirschwasser

1 pound bittersweet chocolate for dipping

1. Grind the nuts in a food processor (a blender will probably not grind the nuts fine enough) until the oil in them starts to be released, they seem moist, and, when pressed between your fingers, keep their shape. This process takes longer for almonds than for walnuts.

2. Place the fondant and the flavoring in the top of a double boiler over medium heat. Melt, and fold the nuts into it.

3. Form into ¾-inch diameter balls.

4. Temper the chocolate and dip each ball into it (see Techniques).

5. Store unrefrigerated, but in a cool place, well sealed from light and moisture. These truffles are suitable for freezing.

VARIATION

Add 2 tablespoons unsweetened cocoa to the fondant melting in the double boiler.

OPTIONAL
GARNISHES

32 blanched almonds
Threads of white chocolate (page 41).

Chocolate-covered Marzipan II

This recipe uses plain granulated sugar instead of fondant, so it is not quite as smooth, but very good if you don't have fondant on hand.

8 ounces blanched almonds or walnuts
1 cup sugar
½ to 1 egg white, lightly beaten

1. Grind the nuts in a food processor as described in preceding recipe.

2. Blend the nuts and sugar, adding only enough egg white to moisten and bind them together.

Follow steps 3, 4, and 5 in preceding recipe. These truffles are suitable for freezing.

GARNISHES

Royal Icing

....
100 ONE-
QUARTER-INCH
FLOWERETS

These garnishes must be made at least a day ahead so they can dry out, but they keep for 6 months.

1¼ cups sifted and then measured powdered sugar
¼ teaspoon cream of tartar
2 tablespoons egg white (about 1 egg)

....

Food coloring

1. Sift the powdered sugar and cream of tartar together. Whisk the egg whites a bit and then add the sugar. If it is very humid, the mixture may take more sugar; add a tablespoon at a time. If it seems too dry and stiff, add a little more egg white (not water). The mixture should be stiff enough to hold its shape when piped from a pastry bag, but not so stiff that it is difficult to squeeze it through the bag.

2. Divide into as many portions as you want colors and add the coloring. A drop or two should be enough.

3. Place in a pastry bag fitted with a floweret or leaf tip and pipe the desired shapes onto wax or parchment paper. Set in a cool, dry place to harden uncovered before removing from the paper.

4. When completely hard (they will seem rocklike), wrap in a plastic bag and store well sealed from light and moisture.

Candied Citrus Rind

Very easy to make and a million times tastier than the dried-out leathery rinds sold in supermarkets. This recipe is a formula and can be made with any amount of rind.

Rind
Sugar
Citrus juice

1. Prepare the rind by washing the fruit, peeling, and then removing all the white inner skin. Cut into thin strips (1/16 inch). Measure the rind. Pour boiling water over it and drain.

2. Measure an amount each of sugar and citrus juice that is double the amount of rind; for example, 2 cups sugar and 2 cups juice for 1 cup rind. In a heavy saucepan, place the sugar and juice and bring to a boil. Add the rind and cook until all the syrup is absorbed. Take care that the sugar doesn't burn; it can happen very quickly.

3. Roll the rind in additional sugar and dry 24 hours before wrapping and storing in a cool place.

Candied Flower Petals

A colorful and tasty garnish. Be sure you do not use any flowers that are poisonous or have been treated with insecticide.

Flower petals (roses, violets, nasturtiums, etc.)
Egg whites
Sugar

1. Rinse any dust off the petals. Lightly beat the egg whites and brush them over the petals. Sprinkle sugar over the petals.

2. Place on wax or parchment paper and dry in a safe place for 24 hours. Store well sealed away from light and moisture.

MAIL-ORDER GUIDE

Bissinger's
205 West Fourth Street
Cincinnati, Ohio 45202

Chocolate mill, a gadget for making chocolate curls

The Godiva Boutique by Mail
P.O. Box 535
Clinton, Connecticut 06413

"Godiva Sweetened Chocolate for the Kitchen"

Istanbul Express
2432 Durant Avenue
Berkeley, California 94704

Excellent selection of chocolate available in bulk

Levkar by the Barrel
H. Roth and Son
1577 First Avenue
New York, New York 10028

Excellent selection of equipment and ingredients

Maid of Scandinavia
3244 Raleigh Avenue
Minneapolis, Minnesota 55416

Equipment and ingredients

Murray Brothers
11256 Cornell Drive
Cincinnati, Ohio 45242

Candy making supplies and ingredients

Narsai's Market
389 Colusa Avenue
Berkeley, California 94707
Baking chocolate available in bulk

Paprikas Weiss Importer
1546 Second Avenue
New York, New York 10028
Ingredients and some equipment

Williams-Sonoma
Mail Order Department
P.O. Box 3792
San Francisco, California 94119
Equipment and excellent selection of baking
chocolate

Wilton Enterprises
2240 West 75th Street
Woodridge, Illinois 60515
Candy making supplies and ingredients

Or, look in the Yellow Pages of your local telephone directory under "Candy and Confectionery Supplies" or "Cake Decorating Supplies."

INDEX